THE PHOENIX CUPS®

A CUP FILLING STORY

Discover your personal needs for fulfilment;
because you can't pour from an empty cup

SANDI & CHRISTOPHER PHOENIX

Second edition revised

Published by Phoenix Support Publishing
PO Box 2112 Wellington Point
Queensland 4160 Australia

© 2023 Phoenix Cups IP Holdings Pty Ltd. ACN 633 355 487

Trademarks in this book consist of:
The Phoenix Cups®
Connection Cup®
Safety Cup®
Mastery Cup®
Fun Cup®
Freedom Cup®
Will to Fill™
Skill to Fill™

All rights reserved. No part of this publication may be reproduced, distributed, or transmitted in any form or by any means, including photocopying, recording, or other electronic or mechanical methods, without the prior written permission of the publisher, except in the case of brief quotations embodied in critical reviews and certain other non-commercial uses permitted by copyright law. For permission requests write to the publisher, addressed "Attention: Permissions Coordinator," at the address below.

ISBN: 978-0-6487058-1-9

Ordering information

Contact the publisher:
Call 1300 361 243
Email hello@phoenixcups.com.au
Visit www.phoenixcups.com.au

For Dionne,
Atreyu, Grace,
Lucy, and Koby

AUTHOR'S NOTE
CHRISTOPHER PHOENIX

On November 18, 1988, Steven Spielberg and George Lucas released an animated film about an orphaned dinosaur called The Land Before Time. Prior to its release, the hype in the school playground, and among my fellow grade two peers, was immense. Children met under monkey bars and at the bottom of metal slides to discuss the film's cover image of a menacing T-Rex, and the lovable junior dinosaurs. My pals Brian, with his fiery red hair and freckles, and Damian, with his buck teeth and bowl cut, invited me to go to the weekend screening with them. I declined the invite, saying, in an off-hand way, that my older brother was going to take me.

The buzz paid off for Spielberg and Lucas, as the film grossed over eighty four million dollars in the box office; a considerable achievement for an animated film in 1988. When my pals returned after the weekend, they were ecstatic. The excitement they felt, however, belonged to them alone. My brother didn't take me to the movie that weekend – it was really never an option. At that time my family was financially unstable. I just didn't want my friends to know.

Since I couldn't afford to go see the movie, I took what information I could from the conversations of the other children and began picturing the film in my mind. I then wrote my own version. Once I finished writing that story, I plagiarised the characters, and created more stories. After a time, I grew excited about my newfound ability to use words to conjure up images, create sensations, develop worlds, and began creating my own characters and narratives. Not only did my family's financial setback help me to discover my love for writing, it was also writing that helped me fill my extremely large Freedom Cup. I could now transport myself anywhere I wanted to be. The written word had freed me. I have been an avid writer ever since.

A strange and curious thing then happened in June 2014 during one of my writing sessions. I penned a character named Sandy, who had a tangled mess of wavy amber hair, and whose gypsy jewellery danced musically from her wrists. Sandy had a fondness for red sangria and would pick out the fruit with her delicate fingers. In November of that same year, I met and fell madly in love with Sandi Phoenix, who was every bit, and more, of the Aphrodite I'd conceived. When we met, she introduced me to the foundations of her Cups theory. Since then, we've developed the Phoenix Cups to how it currently stands, and continue to present the theoretical framework in workshops, conferences, and through written resources all around the globe.

I want to thank the entire Phoenix Support team, as well as anyone who has been a part of the journey getting this book and framework to where it is today. Kit Carstairs, you are a Rockstar editor! Your feedback has been invaluable and has made this book so much greater. Jodi Duncan, you saw our vision, helped us sharpen it, and brought it to life beautifully. I also want to provide a special thank you to Natalie, not only did she help me with my craft, she also helped me overcome the toughest period of my life, and I am forever thankful to her. I must also thank every philosopher who has ever calmed, excited, expanded, and confused my brain. And of course, my biggest thank you goes to Sandi, who is my love, my inspiration, my wife, and my hero.

AUTHOR'S NOTE
SANDI PHOENIX

I am writing this introduction because I need to tell you a secret before you read this book. Hidden in this story is another story. My story. To date, it is a secret known only by those close to me. It is the tale of the origin of the name Phoenix, and the calamity that sparked it. I personally wrote Chapter 20 (The Presentation), through a stream of hot tears, tapping away at my laptop, on the beautiful island of Bali. My husband, Chris, was working beside me, not speaking, but every now and then would put his hand on my shoulder, or gently wipe my tears. Chapter 20 is the keynote I've always wanted to deliver on one of the many stages I've presented on, but I couldn't quite bring myself to be that vulnerable. Or, risk bursting into big ugly crying in front of hundreds of people. So, before I find the courage to do that, I've told it within the pages of this book, in the hope that it inspires you, or validates you and your story. But no cheating! Resist the urge to jump ahead. This story is purposefully placed toward the back of the book and jumping to it won't do it justice.

Chris came into my world in 2014. He not only changed my life, but also the lives of so many others who he has delivered the Phoenix Cups framework to, through either fascinating keynotes, interactive workshops, or online content. At the end of 2018, Chris pleaded with me to write a book about the Phoenix Cups. I told him I had no idea where to start, and asked him to use his creative writing talent to give it a go. As it turns out, he nailed it. Not only did he do the framework justice, but he gave it life through a tangible story, filled with eccentric – yet endearing – characters. Of course, the only real character in the story is myself, and Chris' idealisation of me is evident in the way he portrays me. This book is a collection of our thoughts, told skilfully by my husband, woven together with dashes of psychology, and a great deal of the philosophies that make his eyes sparkle when he speaks of them.

Chris' contribution, as well as that of the awesome team members (past and present) at Phoenix Support, especially Tara Hill and Bronwyn Ball, and that of my colleague and mentor, Dr Louise Porter, have made the Phoenix Cups framework deeper, richer, and oh-so inspiring. I have a much longer list of thank yous and acknowledgements that I've posted on our website. I am forever grateful to everyone who has come along for the ride. And I want to thank you, too, for coming along. So, buckle up, and let's get started.

DISCLAIMER

The main characters and events that take place in this story are fictional. With the exception of Chapter 20, names, characters, businesses, places, events, locales, and incidents are either the products of the author's imagination or used in a fictitious manner. Any resemblance to actual persons, living or dead, or actual events is purely coincidental. This book is not intended as a substitute for medical or psychological advice. The reader should regularly consult a professional in matters relating to their health.

CONTENTS

1. The Beginning is the End is the Beginning — 10
2. Thus, Spoke the Phoenix — 14
3. About a Girl — 18
4. Father of Mine — 24
5. The Safety Cup — 27
6. The Will to Fill — 39
7. Yesterday's Pain — 47
8. The Connection Cup — 51
9. Cup-filling Mischief — 61
10. Until it Sleeps — 65
11. The Mastery Cup — 69
12. Even if you never saw it — 79
13. The Freedom Cup — 82
14. Road to Nowhere — 96
15. The Soft Parade — 101
16. The Fun Cup — 107
17. Cups and Responsibility — 119
18. Acceptance, Meaning and Gratitude — 132
19. Past and Present — 143
20. The Presentation — 146
21. Blinded by the Light — 156
22. Children of the Revolution — 159
23. Parting Ways — 164
24. The End is the Beginning is the End — 168

JACK

1. THE BEGINNING IS THE END IS THE BEGINNING

Beep.

Beep.

Beep.

'How long does it take for the heart to stop beating?' I ask, standing over my father.

Beep.

'It depends how strong it is,' the nurse replies.

Outside in the night sky the rain falls sideways, while I look down at the old man in the bed, with the dark sunken eyes and open mouth.

Beep.

'Can he still hear me now?' I ask.

'I like to think he can.'

Beep.

'I suppose it doesn't matter,' I sigh.

'Sorry?' the nurse asks, and I shake my head.

In the next bed over, behind the blue plastic curtain, comes a man's gravelly voice, 'If it means anything, my father didn't love me much either.'

Beep.

'Please excuse Frank,' the nurse smiles. 'He often chats with himself… or to his daughter.'

The skin on my father's face has turned from olive to grey. His lips are dry and cracked, and he looks all nose and earlobes.

'Can I get you anything?' the nurse asks. I shake my head. She smiles politely and leaves the room.

I take a seat beside my father's bed; how different he looks. I remember as a child how strong I thought he was. He'd hold a coin in his fist with the challenge that if I could pry it open I could have it. Not even with two hands could I get that fist to open. Even today I don't know if I feel as strong as he was back then. When I look at him now, all atrophied, it looks as though someone has embalmed his skeleton. The last time we spoke was nearly a decade ago. How plump his cheeks were then. How sallow they are now.

Beep.

'I'm dying too,' the man behind the curtain says, 'but it's fine.'

Should I have come up and seen him while he was still conscious? Should I even be here now? Apart from my brother, I doubt he's had any other visitors.

'The damndest thing is, by the time I had found peace, it was too late. But it's okay. In the end it's all okay,' the man continues.

Everything about this room is uninviting. The grey vinyl armchair I'm sitting in and the beige plastic bed table can all be sanitised in moments, letting you know your stay will not be too long. Even the untouched, watered-down green jelly says: 'Don't get too comfortable'.

'Do you want to know the secret to making everything okay?' the man asks.

Would my father even want me here?
Beep.

'Well do you?'

'Who are you talking to?' I explode, and for some reason point to my chest even though he can't see me through the curtain.

'Who the hell else do you think I am talking to?'

For a moment all that can be heard is the rain tapping on the window and the dull howling of the wind.

'Well, do you want to know the secret to fulfilment?'

I don't want to deal with this old man right now, or even the crazy man behind the curtain.

'I'm not saying it's something you'll achieve, but it's something I'd like to tell you about. It's not this "cup half-full, half-empty" kinda thing... not exactly.' His voice suddenly sharpens, 'What? What did you say? No Darlene, I am not boring this young man.'

I go to peer around the curtain to see if there is someone else in the room with him. As I move in my seat, out of the corner of my eye it looks as though my father's top lip quivers, and it pulls my attention. Silence befalls us, this time it lasts from the time the long hand of the clock moves from the seven to the nine.

Beep.

I remember once when I was six and was watching my father sleeping on the couch. I remember the way his eyelids seemed to protrude as if his eyeballs were too large. This was the second time I had come to visit him since my mother moved us to the other side of the country. Looking at his face now, those eyelids don't seem as big. If anything, they have sunken further into his skull.

'Okay, we've discussed it and since neither of us are going anywhere soon, we've decided to tell you about the Cups,' the old man says. 'You've heard the saying "You can't pour from an empty cup"? We connect with this phrase, don't we? Sometimes we feel like we've got nothing left and need to refill. But what is it, this cup that we seem to notice most when it's bone dry?'

I stay quiet and hope that he stops talking soon.

'Are you ready for a great big light-bulb moment, son?' he says. 'Are you ready to see your own behaviours, and those of the people around you, in a whole new light?

Beep.

'Are you ready to have your world changed forever?'

Beep.

'Here it is. The big news. Your life-changing moment…'

Beep.

'You don't have one Cup.'

Beep.

'You have five Cups.'

Beep.

'Each Cup represents different basic human life needs that we all have. Fulfilment is the active potential to fill those five Cups.'

Beep.

'But before I tell you what each Cup is, what it represents in terms of your life needs, or how this all relates to taking ownership of your life. Let me tell you first how I came to know about the Phoenix Cups.'

FRANK

2. THUS, SPOKE THE PHOENIX

Reaching into my coat jacket I take out a hip flask, and throw some down my throat. The liquid wets my tongue, but I can't tell if it's whiskey or bourbon. I look up at a great building in front of me, marvelling at its construction of tinted windows rather than solid walls. I walk up the stairs towards the doors, stopping now and then to catch my breath as I cling to the cold metal railing. I glance down at my wristwatch – 9:37am – before opening the heavy glass doors. A current of warm air hits me in the face as I enter the foyer. Looking left and right, the vastness of the halls quickens my heart. How many lecture rooms can one convention centre hold? How far would I have to walk? A passing usher must have sensed my disorientation. He looks at my ticket and points me to an escalator.

At the top, hundreds of people are gathered. Some chatter with those they arrived with, while others, like myself, stand awkwardly alone. Ten minutes pass before the doors are opened. After I find my seat I take another swig from my flask and then watch as the room fills around me. The house lights are dimmed and a hush falls over the auditorium. A woman with long hazel curls strolls onto the lit stage in front of us.

'Hi, I'm Sandi Phoenix,' she says through a wide smile.

Even from my seat toward the back of the room, I can see that she emanates power. She moves around the stage like a solo actor might during a Shakespearean soliloquy, telling a heart-wrenching tale of a child labelled the 'naughty kid'. A child whose weekend was wrought with visions of domestic violence, fear, and despair. She speaks in great detail of the tragedy this boy experiences that will never be seen by those who judge him the most for his behaviours.

I'm enamoured by her confident voice that holds the complete attention of every one of the thousand people in her audience. Every pause, pitch and hand gesture moves us so that at times we laugh, while other times we weep. Most importantly, by the time she stops speaking, we're transformed.

I found my way into her conference on children's behaviour not at all expecting my life to change. I'd gone seeking different answers. Not for myself, but for my grandchild – even though my daughter hadn't spoken to me in years I'd heard she was having issues with her son. Some part of me believed that if I could just help her with his behaviour, then perhaps she'd have me back in her life.

On stage, as the light shimmers on Sandi's hair, she falls silent. She scans her audience almost like a bird of prey, patiently preparing for the best moment to change tone and pace. You could hear a pin drop in the room – I am sure I am not the only one with my mouth gaping.

Sandi takes a few steps closer to the front of the stage. 'Imagine human behaviour is motivated by five basic human life needs. These include the need for safety, the need for connection, the need for freedom, the need for mastery, and the need for fun. The difference between us is that we all have different sized needs. Where one person may have a big need for connection, another person may have a smaller need for connection. Because of these different sized needs, differing amounts of these needs being met, and differing behavioural choices, their behaviours to meet their needs would be different.'

Using an analogy about Cups, Sandi paints a picture of how humans have five metaphorical Cups that represent these basic human life needs. The size of their individual Cups represents how much of each need they have. While the fullness or emptiness of their Cups represents how much each need is met or not met.

This analogy gives me a moment of clarity about human behaviour that I'd never before had. I could visualise different people's Phoenix Cups Profiles and suddenly I understand why individuals are motivated to behave the way they do. It's to fill their Cups. Never had the world of psychology held so much interest for me. I was captivated. It was as though some imaginary veil had fallen from my eyes, and I was looking at the world around me for the first time. I was excited. A million questions were swimming about in my brain. I needed to know more.

When Sandi finishes her presentation, she leaves the stage to a deafening applause. I watch as she embraces a man in the wings, and then ducks out of sight. I leave the auditorium and walk into the great hall where there's a banner stand that reads Phoenix Cups. Behind the stand are two women; a petite blonde with a warm smile and a brunette lady. They both emanate warmth as they greet the delegates flocking to the stand to buy resources and ask questions. The stand is busy and I don't feel like battling the crowds to get to the women. Like some kind of magic, the man who embraced Sandi on the edge of the stage walks toward me. I grab him by the arm as he walks by. I am surprised by my own abruptness.

'I'm sorry sir,' I say, 'I didn't mean to take hold of you like that. I'm just so intrigued and my head is swimming. I have so many questions to ask. I need to know so much more.'

The man smiles at me, reaches down, grabs a small booklet and holds it out to me. 'Use this as well as the quiz on our website to determine your own Needs Profile and work out what size your individual Cups are. You can then design a Cup-filling plan. Try to find ways to fill your Cups without affecting the rights and needs of others. And where possible, try to understand other people's needs. Their behaviour is driven by their own Cups.'

His words sound so matter of fact. It's clear he's used to delivering this information, and in the shortest time possible. Looking around me at the hordes of people, I can see why. But something changes suddenly in his demeanour. He looks me over and gives me an almost all-knowing smile. Taking a pen from the table, he turns over a Cups leaflet and scribbles something on the back.

'Find these authors, theorists, and ideas,' he says, handing me the flyer. 'But when you do, keep the Cups in mind. The Phoenix Cups are life affirming. It's about finding fulfilment in this life and in this moment. Only you can fill your Cups. Only you can create your own meanings.'

FRANK

3. ABOUT A GIRL

On the train ride home I devour the information in the booklet, which summarises the framework, and includes an exercise to help determine my own Needs Profile. I turn my attention to the note the man scribbled on the flyer. It's half an A4 page, and the handwriting is barely legible. On it are names like Aurelius, Frankl, and Sisyphus. There are statements I barely understand, like: 'Condemned to be Free', and 'Amor Fati'.

The man's last sentence plays over in my mind: Only you can fill your Cups. Only you can create your own meanings.

I'd have to do some research.

Taking my phone from my pocket, I dial my daughter's phone number. I am excited to think I finally have some guidance for her son's behaviour. The sound on the other end of the line suggests that the phone is disconnected – Darlene has probably forgotten to pay her phone bill again.

The train carriage sways gently, and the lights flicker as we pass through a tunnel. Its rhythm, as it glides along the tracks, lulls me into a daydream. I remember a time when I was in Uluwatu, on the west coast of southern Bali. Darlene must've been six or seven years old. As we strolled through the markets a pink ukulele, which hung from a wall, caught her eye. The Indonesian man in the stall followed her gaze, took the instrument down, and strummed some soothing chords.

'Daddy, look,' she said.

I bartered with the man, but he wouldn't take my highest price.

'I'm sorry baby,' I said to Darlene, 'it's too expensive.'

'Okay Daddy,' she said, and lowered her head.

Even though Darlene accepted the disappointment, heavy hands seemed to push down upon my shoulders. As she walked into another stall with her mother, I turned around and went back to the man and paid him what he asked. When Darlene came back out of the shop and saw the ukulele in my hands, her face turned as bright as the Bali sun.

The daydream is broken when the train conductor calls out 'Central Station. End of the line.' I realise that I caught the wrong train and am now in the city. I don't know what propels me, but instead of changing platforms and catching another train home, I decide to get out and wander through the streets and laneways of the city of Brisbane.

Walking around with this new-found philosophical frame-work it is as if something has cleared the air. I feel like I am seeing the world for the first time in my sixty-seven years. Not only do I people-watch, contemplating their Cups, I marvel at the great cathedrals, awe at the engineering of those towering bridges, and am enthralled by all the modern street art I had once dismissed as graffiti vandalism. I become alive to my senses, and what comes to mind is Oscar Wilde's account of his protagonist curing his soul by means of his senses. But there is no debauchery here; my senses are filling my Cups. I am drinking in my world as though it were an elixir. I must've looked like a fool with my neck craned skywards and a dumb look on my face, but I didn't care. I don't know if I'd ever been so in the moment as I was during that walk. Even though I'd walked for nearly an hour, my frailty had only allowed me to travel four blocks.

So, it is with my neck craned that I first see the signage of the book store. On black hooks, protruding from the stone wall, is a wooden sign with the words Dan's Books scorched into the cedar.

Stepping over the stone footing, I enter the shop, which no longer has walls but rows of book spines. The worn carpet guides the labyrinth of nooks and crannies. The store has a musty scent that I instantly associate with knowledge and comfort. At the counter stands a petite woman with silver hair in a bun, she's wearing a cotton dress with faded sunflowers on it. The dress must've been so old that the yellow of the petals look like butter-oil drops. Her hands are thin and delicate as she places a customer's leather-bound book inside a cotton shoulder bag and hands it over.

I explore my way through the shop of new and second-hand books and stop at a copy of Richard Yates' short stories on loneliness, which I'd read as a younger man – how nostalgic those stories are for me. Tales of despair that somehow made me feel much less alone when I understood that the personal is in fact the universal.

I must've been staring at the cover for some time when the bookkeeper calls in a sharp tone, 'Can I help you?'

I turn to see her chin slightly raised, with her face as still as marble. An awkward pause comes between us – well, awkward for me. I fumble with my pocket until I pull out the flyer with the scribbled notes. I hand it to her at arm's length, as though she were a fierce beast that I was attempting to feed.

'Does any of this mean anything to you?' I ask. 'I want to do some research.'

She studies the note, and then peers off to the left as though she's forgotten I am there. 'Some of these are authors, though some of this refers to concepts, not book titles… I can probably point you in the right direction.' She traces her index finger along a sentence on the page. 'I don't see the correlations here though. In fact, some of this seems downright contradictory. Where did you get this?' she asks, still not looking at me.

'A man at a conference gave it to me. I'd just heard his partner spea…'

'I hope you weren't expecting any light reading.'

Without a word, she scuttles her way through the warren and stops at a shelf in a claustrophobic corner. She kneels down in front of the books and runs her fingers along the top of the spines, as though the book covers are brail, until she finds what she's looking for. With the same finger, she hooks the top of the book and pulls it out.

'Start with this,' she says.

The book is thin and has a worn brown cover. There's no dust jacket, only the faded gilt word Meditations written across the front. I flick the volume open and skim a few pages and find a series of journal entries, sometimes long passages, while other times short three or four sentence statements. There are even a few single sentence epigrams. I read one aloud, 'Men are born for the sake of each other. So either teach or tolerate.'

I peer up from the page and notice the bookkeeper studying me, as though she's suspicious. 'What's in your hands is the private journal of one of history's greatest rulers. He was a Roman Emperor who upheld incredible integrity, where so many others with absolute power had disgraced themselves. His journal is a work of humility, discipline, and kindness. It is an incredible resource of guidance and wisdom. Why did the man who gave you this paper ask you to read this?'

'Well,' I say, 'this morning I was at a conference. The speaker – Sandi Phoenix – introduced us to something called the Phoenix Cups. Building upon, and adapting the work of a theorist called Dr William Glasser, she said as human beings we all have basic human life needs. She says that we all have a Safety Cup, a Connection Cup, a Mastery Cup, a Freedom Cup, and what was the last one? Oh yeah, a Fun Cup. But she said, we all have different sized Cups, which make up our own unique profile. She also said that as human beings, every behaviour we choose is to fill one of these Cups.'

I spend the next ten minutes telling the bookkeeper every aspect I could recall of the Cups, including what needs they represent, and what behaviours fill them. Like a child recounting their day to a parent, with all the untapped enthusiasm, I course my way through the theoretical framework, at times muddling up timelines, theorists, or correct pronunciations, until eventually I feel satisfied that I've said all that I can.

'So, I guess, we all have a different Cups Profile, or different sized Cups, and every behaviour we do is to meet a need – or fill a Cup. Sandi said when a person has full Cups, or knows how to fill their Cups, they feel good and have a strong sense of fulfilment. When their Cups are emptying, a person feels unease and is driven to choose behaviours that will fill their Cups.'

The bookkeeper's face remains unchanged, and I wonder if she's heard a word of my speech. 'What was it that the man said to you as he passed you the piece of paper?'

'He said, "Only you can fill your Cups. Only you can create your own meanings."'

She looks back at the piece of paper in her hands and re-reads his scribbles. 'I see,' she says still looking at the paper. 'He can't give you the answers because filling your Cups is an individual experience, and it's your own responsibility. What he's saying is no one can fill your Cups but you.' She darts past me suddenly, into another section of her shop. This time the book she's reaching for is above shoulder height. She flicks through the pages and then reads in silence in front of me for what feels like a full minute.

'So, this is Dan's store?' I ask, forcing conversation.

'It is,' she replies not taking her eyes off her page.

'I like his store.'

'Her store.'

'You're Dan?'

'Yes, Danielle. Call me Dan,' she says as she flicks through some more pages until she finds another passage to read in its entirety. 'No, this isn't the one,' she says, putting it back on the shelf. She turns to face me, and for the first time since we met, I feel acknowledged by her. At first she says nothing, and again I sense that she's untrusting of me.

'Where do you live?' she finally asks.

'A few train stops from here.'

'If you come back tomorrow afternoon, I'll compile a list of some books I think you'll need. Are you able to leave me this?' she asks, holding up the piece of paper.

JACK

4. FATHER OF MINE

Beep.
Beep.
Beep.

The man behind the curtain stops speaking directly to me and begins to mumble, making me realise how intently I've been listening to his story. Beep.

I look at my father's face, and even in unconsciousness his eyebrows push tightly together. That same expression takes me back to when I was a boy living across the other side of the country. My only contact with him then was a birthday card, and a week's holiday at his home over the Christmas break. Whenever I think of that week with him, I remember the faded, cracked mustard vinyl seats of the taxi he owned. I remember splaying out along that back seat, alone, with the hot sun heating my small legs, waiting for him while he spent hours inside that strange building. The seat would soon get too hot and I would have to jump into the front. When the boredom became unbearable, I'd get out and cross the hot tar and enter the building. There I would find my father with small bits of paper in his hands, smoking cigarettes, and with that same strained expression, staring intently up at the televisions on the wall, where there were images of horses galloping along with small colourful men on their backs.

'Can we go soon?' I'd ask.

'Five more minutes,' he'd reply, not taking his eyes off the screen.

I don't know how many times I'd hear him say 'five more minutes' before he actually meant it. Sometimes the sun would be starting to set before that five minutes was finally up. My older brother had seen the pointlessness of the yearly trip before I had and didn't bother coming anymore. I can still feel the hot vinyl backseat of that taxi.

Beep.

'Okay, Darlene wants me to stop talking, but I think I need to tell you more,' says the man, breaking through my reverie. 'Tell me son, what's your name?'

I shake my head to myself and instead of answering I take my phone from my pocket.

'Shy one, hey? Well, I'm never short of a word,' he says, and begins to ramble.

I send my brother a message: *Does the old man in the next bed ever shut up?*

I try to look out the window, but because it is so bright in the room, I'm startled by my own reflection. A foot away from my own face, I am suddenly aware of my appearance as though I am truly looking at it for the first time. This is how others must see me. The real me. It is as though somehow my bathroom mirror has been lying to me all this time. Perhaps it is because whenever I look at that reflection I prepare myself with the face I want to portray. Sitting here now, unprepared, this window is far more sobering. Who is this forty-year-old man staring back at me? Has his nose always been this wide? His eyes this weary? His brown hairline this receding? I can't help now but think, how did I get to be here? What happened to the exuberant young Jack? Jack, the engineer who transcended his low socio-economic background. Jack, the proud father of two beautiful little boys. Jack, the strong... To be fair though, was that ever the real Jack? Have I ever spent a day at that job without the crippling anxiety of imposter syndrome? Was my time with my sons that long before their mother found a new husband? Have I ever really been strong, or have I always been a self-doubting coward?

My phone vibrates. There's a message from my brother: *You mean Frank? Trust me, you won't shut him up so don't even try. He's actually a good man. Listen in, he has some valuable things to say.*

FRANK

5. THE SAFETY CUP

The next afternoon at 4:11pm I find my way back to Dan's bookstore. Stopping out the front, I look up again at the cedar shop sign, marvelling at the craftsmanship. I take a small sip from my flask before entering. Dan's serving a customer when I arrive, but she must've seen me in the corner of her eye. She waves me over without a break in her conversation and I wait patiently nearby until she's finished. When her customer leaves, Dan looks me over as peculiarly as she did the day before. The same unease creeps into my belly.

'Come with me,' she says when she's ready.

Dan invites me behind the counter and through the faded purple cotton tapestry hanging in the doorway, blocking the hall behind from customers. Halfway down the hall, on the left, is an open door. As we enter the room the shop bell from the front door jingles.

'Take a seat. I won't be long,' she says and ducks back out of the room.

I look at my surroundings with all the freedom of someone not being watched. The room is dimly lit by a dull yellow light shining from the bulb above, which has no cover. There's a window, but thick heavy drapes are pulled across. Catalogues and other junk mail pile up on the floor in the corner. On the back wall stands a small bookshelf with a series of moleskin notebooks on them, and nearby there's a sink with a white electric kettle, and a small cupboard above it. In the middle of the room there's an old round wooden table with six or seven books, a notepad, some butcher's paper and some markers strewn across it. Through the door I hear Dan talking to her customer, and every now and then I hear feigned laughter. After a few moments she returns, and noticing that I am still standing, she motions for me to take a seat at the table, while she deliberately separates us by taking a seat a space apart.

There's something peculiar about her mannerism that I can't quite put my finger on. Where yesterday she was composed, almost domineering, today there's a strange wistfulness about her. Not that I know her at all, but she has all the manic gestures of someone who hasn't slept. Meanwhile, I slept more peacefully than I have in years, and have remained relatively sober.

'So yesterday was a little odd wasn't it?' she said. 'I realised after you left that I didn't catch your name?'

'It's Frank,' I say.

'So, Frank, I must say when I closed the store yesterday, and went looking for the books and authors on your list, I couldn't help but become more intrigued by these Cups. So much so that I did a little research and looked up their website.'

'And what are your thoughts?'

'Well, I'm not sure just yet. Anyway, here are your books,' she says, placing her hand on the pile at the centre of the table. She looks at the hand-written note again. 'Frank,' she says, still looking at the note, 'it would be fine by me if you'd like to hang out here and study. In fact, I think I'd like to learn more about these Cups myself,' she lifts her head and looks me in the eye. 'Would you mind if I look into the Cups with you?'

I nod. 'I would appreciate it very much if you could. I am an old man so I could use all the help I can get.'

'What if we met each day and looked into each Cup individually?'

Although her eyes are drawn, there's still a level of exuberance in the way she speaks. It's as if she required the night to digest all she'd learnt. Dan's enthusiasm, languid as it is, is contagious. I am thrilled that she not only provided all the resources I need but that she also wants to be part of this journey.

'Where should we start?' I ask.

For the first time, I witness the corners of her mouth lift. 'Oh, you want to start today? Okay, well if so, I think we should start at the Safety Cup – after all, it's the closest Cup that would represent the base level in Maslow's hierarchy.'

'I'm in,' I reply.

'Well,' she says, 'let's get started, shall we? Okay, according to your recount of the lady on stage…'

'Sandi Phoenix.'

'… she said you can often determine a person's dominant Cup, or Cups they are currently filling, by their behaviours. I say we start by brainstorming what we think fits into the Safety Cup, and then what we think are the behaviours people may choose to fill it.'

Dan pulls over a piece of butcher's paper, and taking a black marker, writes the words Safety Cup in the centre, and circles it.

'Okay,' she says, 'you heard the woman's presentation. What words come to mind when you think of the Safety Cup?'

I falter for a moment. Dan's clearly more educated than I am, which makes me a little hesitant. 'Umm, food, shelter, rest, wellness…' I suggest.

'Great,' she says and, for the second time today, smiles. With a purple marker, she writes the words on the page, then turns her expectant stare back to me.

'Umm, predictability even?'

She stops writing. 'Interesting. Predictability is a psychological need. Maslow's base need was purely physiological, as was Dr William Glasser's need for survival in his Choice Theory. We can see the Safety Cup, however, is both physiological and psychological. What other psychological behaviours do you think fill the Safety Cup?'

'What about trust and stability?'

Dan smiles again, and my chest lifts. I assume this is what pride feels like.

'Now, describe to me what you'd imagine someone with a dominant Safety Cup to be like?'

'Hmmm,' I say. As I ponder, I feel Dan's stare on me. 'Okay, when I think of someone with a dominant Safety Cup my daughter, Darlene, comes to mind.' A warmth fills my heart just thinking of Darlene. It amazes me how my thoughts alone might fill my Connection Cup.

'When I think of her behaviours, I mostly think of her need for sleep. She must get at least eight hours sleep at night, if not more. If she has any less, she gets incredibly grumpy. On the weekend she also naps during the day. Boy, can she nap. I'm not talking about five or ten minutes. She can nap for over an hour. Let's see. She also loves to watch hours-upon-hours of television. I reckon she would nearly spend the entire day on the couch watching television if she could.'

'Ah, she is a TV binger. That's what my husband used to call it,' Dan says.

'Let's see, what else. Okay, she needs her food as well, but not in the same sense I do. When I eat, I eat for pleasure. She eats almost out of necessity. Three meals a day in fact. And if she's ever late eating, she gets very annoyed. She once told me that my forgetting to eat is a special kind of stupid.

The funny thing is, at one stage she had a weight issue and was constantly eating foods that were no good for her. Eventually, she went on a health kick and lost all her weight. Her desire for food though is still there. Now she just eats lots of healthy foods instead.'

Although Dan's mouth doesn't move, her eyes widen, and for the first time I feel some warmth arise from her.

'Her health-food kick actually also kick-started her fitness,' I continue.

'As much as I love her, I used to think she was lazy. Now she's extremely active. Again though, it seems to me that she is doing it to fill her Safety Cup. She now wants to be in control of her health and her body for her safety and security.'

Dan jots down notes on the page, with a pen now rather than the marker.

'Tell me more about her.'

'What else can I tell you? Okay, how about we look at her psychological safety needs. Let me think... Oh yes, where I have done many jobs – and at times worked for myself – she's always been cautious around job security. She's been in the same role for what seems forever, even though it seems to bring her no joy. I'd go as far as saying she hates her job. She has the skill set now to go out and work for herself, but she won't take the plunge. She'd rather the security of a safe and predictable weekly pay-check.'

'What does she do?' Dan asks, with her eyes still on the page.

'Something to do with building approvals... She's actually good at budgeting too, though that can fit in both Safety and Mastery I guess, but I can see her bank savings almost like a squirrel storing away acorns. I sometimes wish I could do that. Oh, and I remember taking her to theme parks when she was young. She would always favour the safer looking rides. She was very risk averse. Her survival's definitely paramount to her...'

Dan stands abruptly and walks over to the kettle and switches it on. As she reaches for a mug she asks, with her back to me, 'So what do you think your daughter's different Cup sizes are?'

'Hmmm, I would say her Safety Cup is her dominant Cup, as well as a big Mastery Cup, since she can be very bossy sometimes. Her Freedom Cup is fairly small, which may have something to do with freedom threatening her Safety Cup? Actually, if I really think about it, her Freedom Cup is not small, it is just empty due to her Safety Cup taking precedence. I remember her once wanting to travel to Japan but she kept talking herself out of it by coming up with different excuses. Silly excuses like she would need more money, yet I know she does very well financially. There's clearly a conflict there between her Safety Cup and her Freedom Cup. What next? Okay, although she doesn't always like to show it, she is a caring person. So, if I had to describe her Cups, I would say her dominant Cup is Safety, with an equally large Mastery Cup. Then, probably a medium sized Freedom Cup, followed by the Connection Cup, and finally the Fun Cup.'

Dan puts down her mug of tea on the table. I wonder for a moment if she'd gestured to see if I wanted a tea as well and I missed it. She picks up the pen and scribbles more notes on the page, and for a brief moment I feel like I'm in a therapy session.

'Does she live here?'

I smile politely and nod. I don't want to tell her that she hasn't spoken to me in half a decade. Dan reaches forward and pulls a hard cover book from the pile on the table.

'Although my husband was the armchair philosopher, there was one great thinker who he introduced me to which I devoured. His name is Arthur Schopenhauer, and I fell in love with him instantly. His philosophy is so pessimistic that it's almost humorous. He was very clever though. Anyway, in this book Schopenhauer argued that all things have a universal Will. He said this Will was a force within us all, which he called the "Will to Life." This fellow believed the Will to Life is an unconscious, non-rational driver we have and need for self-preservation and motivation to survive and reproduce. This book even inspired Charles Darwin and his work on Natural Selection. Anyway, Schopenhauer said the Will to Life results in a kind of suffering to motivate us to continue what I guess we could say are Safety Cup-filling behaviours. So, if we apply the Will to Life with the Phoenix Cups, your Will to Life is only momentarily satisfied when your Safety Cup is full. When it is full there is no more striving. When it is empty, however, we are motivated – via a kind of suffering – to fill it.'

'I've heard the saying "Will to Live" before but never really thought about its origin, or its true meaning. I've heard people say before they've 'given up the will to live', but I think they're referring to giving up trying in life, which is vastly different. It certainly isn't referring to an unconscious driver that is motivating us to choose to fill our Safety Cup.'

'Now, Schopenhauer,' Dan continues, almost as though I hadn't spoken, 'once used the mythological story of Ixion as an analogy to express the Will to Life. Ixion was a king who tried to seduce Zeus' wife. He was punished by being tied to a great wheel that spun for eternity over fire. According to Schopenhauer, when we are driven to satisfy the Will to Life we are in a sense suffering, which we could equate to being turned through the fire. When we think that we are happy or fulfilled, Schopenhauer believes it is just a mistaken, temporary state of non-suffering, when the wheel is not directly over that fire. What I am getting at is if the Will to Life causes us suffering so that we pursue Safety Cup filling, then it is not actually pleasure we feel when the Safety Cup is full, but in a sense, only a lack of the suffering the empty Safety Cup caused.'

Dan is right, this Schopenhauer chap is pessimistic.

'If we relate this back to your daughter, Darlene…' Dan continues, putting both of her palms down on the table. 'You mentioned before how you enjoy eating for pleasure, where she chooses to eat for survival. What I think is that when your daughter was unhealthy, she was eating whatever she could find. She was almost a helpless victim in her Safety Cup filling by letting the Will to Life guide her. Now what I think is happening is that instead of being a helpless victim, who was at the mercy of the Will to Life, Darlene has turned into an activist who chose to dominate the Will to Life, and her Safety Cup, by choosing to eat healthy and exercising.'

'I'm not sure I follow. How do you mean?'

'Well, it's no longer causing her suffering to fill her Safety Cup, or just a lack of suffering with a full Safety Cup when she ate junk food, but instead fulfilment to fill her Safety Cup with exercise and healthy eating. Perhaps the conscious choice to fill all our Cups is just as rewarding? ... Wait, I think I've got it.'

She feverishly writes down the following words as she speaks them: 'Empty Cups is suffering, to motivate us to fill them. Full Cups is merely a lack of that suffering. Perhaps consciously choosing to fill our Cups is fulfilment?' Dan looks up absently as she contemplates her own words. If I could read minds, I would assume she was analysing them for truth.

'Yes,' she says. 'It definitely has to be a conscious choice to fill them. If you consciously fill your Cups you will achieve momentary fulfilment and not just a lack of suffering.'

The same butterflies I felt at the conference when Sandi was speaking start to flutter in my stomach again.

'You know what also comes to mind,' Dan continues, 'is a video clip I saw of a man dying from cancer, and his last lecture on living life. It was as though the appearance of death renewed an appreciation of life's beauty and importance to him. Although the cancer was clearly emptying his Safety Cup, he took more risks and essentially lived life more fully. He gave expression to every form, and even the smallest pleasures seemed to magnify for him. It is curious that this Safety Cup-emptying situation allowed him to truly live.

It seems almost contradictory. It's as though he bucked the Will to Life. He dominated it instead of it dominating him. He won against his nature knowing that keeping the Safety Cup full forever was an impossible task. He chose instead to fill all of his other Cups.'

'I know this one,' I beam. 'It's called *memento mori*. I remember this from art history at school. Our teacher was showing us how so much early art used to include skulls in their paintings. It roughly translates to 'remember death' or remember you must die. My teacher presented it to us, not as a gloomy disclaimer, but to inspire and motivate. A 'carpe diem' kind of thing. That the idea that death looms should motivate you to live now. To not be a slave to the Safety Cup, I guess.'

The shop bell jingles again, Dan's eyebrows tighten, knowing our flow has been interrupted. 'Excuse me Frank,' she says, and leaves the room.

While I wait, I think about Darlene and how obvious it is now that she has a dominant Safety Cup. I wince, remembering how harsh I was with her sometimes. What I thought was pure laziness was just her trying to meet one of her needs. I just didn't understand it because my need for safety isn't as large as hers. I guess it's by understanding someone else's Cups that you can become more tolerant. Perhaps you might not agree with their behaviour, but you can at least now understand why they chose it.

I realise that I've been staring off into space and, as my eyes refocus, I find myself looking at the moleskin notebooks on the bookshelf. My curiosity peaks. What could they be for? Clearly, they're for private use, they're far too small to be bookkeeping ledgers. I listen out and can tell Dan is still helping people in her shop. I'm not sure what wills me, but I go around the table and take the first notebook off the shelf. I sit back down and flick through the pages. They're journal entries. As I start reading the very first entry, I hear Dan's footsteps approaching. I am too far away to put the book back, so I quickly slip it into my coat pocket. When Dan enters the room and takes her seat, she looks wearier than before.

'So, in a nutshell,' she says as she reaches for the pad, and then with the same black pen as before, scribbles down as she speaks: 'A dominant Safety Cup is derived from the Will to Life. Behaviours of a person with a dominant Safety Cup are often physiological, including the need for excess sleeping, eating, and I think possibly a heightened attention to physical safety and even illness.' Dan stops talking suddenly and turns to me, 'I know we didn't discuss this part, but I can't help now thinking back to all my friends who would take the day off work when they were only mildly sick. I once worked six weeks straight with pneumonia.'

She continues writing on the page as she speaks: 'Psychological aspects include the need to feel safe and may present in behaviours such as predictability by maintaining their status quo. A person with a dominant Safety Cup may crave routine, such as regular mealtimes and an approximate bedtime so that they are assured a certain amount of sleep each night. They might prefer to have a plan and are not real fans of going with the flow. Therefore, you could say they are risk averse and prefer predictability. This person does not have to be at the mercy of this Cup, however, as they can fill their Cups in ways that fulfil them, which would be determined individually by the person and by their unique Cups Profile.' Dan stops writing and turns to me. 'Of course, I am generalising a little, and other factors will come into play such as the behaviours driven by the other Cups, which may have a person with a dominant Safety Cup behave differently each time, but I think this is the gist of it. I have a strong feeling that we will be revisiting the Safety Cup as we look at other Cups.'

There's a moment of silence as we contemplate Dan's summary.

'What do you think the Safety Cup is really for?' I ask. 'I mean, I get the Will to Life aspect. But what would you say is the outcome of a full Safety Cup?'

Dan is quiet, staring into space. Just as I go to ask the question again, she says, 'I think the outcome of a full Safety Cup is a sense of security. Yes, that's it. Physiological and psychological security… I guess that's what makes it differ from Dr William Glasser's idea of Survival too.'

Dan raises both sets of fingertips to rub her eyes.

'Why don't we break for a while,' I suggest, 'and go out and get some dinner?'

'We could order in. There is a brilliant Malaysian restaurant who deliver. They do an amazing Roti.'

'How about we go there?' I say.

'Or I could order it, and you go pick it up.'

'I really think we should go out together. Let's get out of this stuffy room for a while.'

'I don't go outside.'

'What do you mean?' I ask.

Her face hardens. 'I said I don't go outside.'

It takes a moment before I realise and I nod apologetically. 'How about we call it an evening?' she says, rustling with the paper on the table and not making eye contact. 'Give me a couple of days and then we can look over the next Cup. Maybe leave your number on the pad. You should go now.'

I scribble down my phone number and give Dan my warmest smile, but she doesn't face me. I leave the shop and she locks the door behind me. I head towards the train station and find I have 16 minutes until the next train. I look at the bar across the street. I could probably fit in one drink before it arrives. Then again, do I really need a drink? My mind feels somewhat clear, unusual for this time of day. Still, one drink couldn't hurt. I've got time. In fact, my train will ensure I only have one drink.

When I enter the bar I hear the jukebox playing, it's a song about an astronaut called Major Tom. The young man behind the bar has a ring through his nose and coloured tattoos up his forearm.

'Whiskey neat,' I say to him, and rest my elbows on the green, odorous bar mat.

'Fix it up now or at the end?' asks the barman as he puts the drink down on a napkin.

'Now,' I say. 'I've got to catch a train in a moment.' I leave a $10 note on the counter, which the barman swaps for a gold coin a moment later. I run my right index finger along the grooves around the glass, all the while wondering why Dan suddenly turned so sallow. Why did she refuse to leave the bookstore, and how long has it been since she last left it?

Some lively people in coloured work vests enter the bar around me. When I turn I feel the notebook shift in my pocket. Damn, I didn't get a chance to put it back. I pull it out and open it up. In the middle of the first page the words read:

Do not read. That means you DANIELLE!

I flick through some more pages. Some are dated at the top right-hand corner while others are blank. The year is always 1992.

Suddenly, I remember my train. Glancing at the clock on the wall, I notice that I only have a few minutes to get back across the street. I don't think I will make it. Instead, I order another drink. Two drinks turn into four or five whiskeys. The sixth, seventh, and eighth drinks are bourbon.

FRANK

6. THE WILL TO FILL

The sound of my TV blaring wakes me up on my couch. I have no memory of coming home, or drinking any of the empty beer cans that litter my coffee table. A melancholy creeps over me as I lay staring at the cartoons. I stare so hard that it's no more than strobing colours. As I wallow in self-pity, I can't help but think of Oscar Wilde, and his position on self-reproach – that it is a luxury. When we blame ourselves, we often feel no one else then has the right to. It's curious how self-pity can be so comforting even though it's destructive.

I roll onto my side and feel something dig into my ribs. I reach into my jacket pocket and pull out the notebook. I lie back and pull apart the covers, flicking through to a random page. I try to make sense of the words, but my eyes won't seem to focus. After a few moments of changing distance the words start to become clear. It's a journal entry dated 22nd August.

Today I asked Dan again if there was anything she wanted for the wedding, and again she said just two things. One, that her parents weren't there. And two, that she wouldn't be wearing a bra. I was impressed that my wife to be has no interest in conventionality and doesn't care too much about weddings, while simultaneously bothered that I am organising the entire thing. She's lucky I love her.

I flick ahead a few more pages in what I can clearly see now is Dan's husband's journal, and the date reads 13th September.

Be with the person who causes you the least amount of pain. Sometimes that person is yourself... Sometimes, however, that person is a stubborn seraph who eats from the street carts of Hoi An without washing her hands first. Sometimes that person is a petite brunette who thinks she's Joan Jett in the shower. Sometimes that person is as tender as peach one minute, and then as ferocious as a kitten the next. What can I say? Although we're all alone, she is the only one I want to share the loneliness with.

As much as I feel like a voyeur, I am intrigued to see a side of Dan that I've not witnessed. What could have happened to steal the sparkle from her eye? I sit up, and with my right foot I knock over a beer can on the floor beside the couch. Instead of picking it up, I watch as it leaks onto the faded brown carpet. I look around the room at all the other empty beer cans. How on earth did I become my father?

My phone rings from somewhere inside the house. I try to ignore it but it keeps on ringing. I curse, pull myself to standing and try to find my phone. It continues to ring and I yell at it to hold on. The moment I find it, next to the stovetop which has on it a pot of uncooked whole potatoes, it stops ringing. I look at the number, but I don't recognise it. Maybe it's Darlene? Maybe this is her new number? The phone beeps to let me know the caller left a message.

'Frank, it's Dan. I don't want you to come into the shop today. I'll call you later, when I am ready for you to come in next.'

Whatever remorse I was feeling for reading the journal ebbs away. Childishly, I rant inside my head: *Fine! I'll stay here and read your husband's journal.* I pull out an opened tin of beans from the fridge – with a cold metal fork still inside it – and take it to the couch. I curse as I step on the wet, beer-stained carpet. I ignore the can still on its side, take a mouthful of beans, then place the tin on the table.

I pick up the journal again and flick it open to the 14th July.
It happened again today. The tissue I coughed into had speckles of red. How strange that death is the one event in life that I ponder the most, that is always the subject of my writing, yet I run from it the moment it presents itself... I introduced Danielle to Sartre today. Sort-of. I just spoke with her about Bad Faith, and his ideas on essence. I don't know any other human on this planet other than Danielle who could arrive so early at liberation and not dread about the possibility of having no inherent meaning. It took me a long time to come to this position. She landed there immediately. I wonder if it is because it was articulated to her by the writings of Sartre, rather than just the existential dread we usually face when we discover our own meaninglessness?... What burdens me these days is quite the opposite. I would find solace in knowing if there was either an inherent meaning or no inherent meaning to life. What really paralyses me is having no answers, of not being able to ever truly know any definitive answers. I even suffer knowing there isn't even truly a way to articulate it if there was a way to know. It's been so debilitating that recently I found myself unable to even get out of bed... but not Danielle. Danielle laughs in the face of the abyss. No dark clammy hand of the unknowable can touch her heart. It's as though she is immune to the despair of the fathomless. What is even more peculiar is that it has nothing to do with ignorance. There is just something about her that seems to be untouchable. She is, despite her canary cage of time and culture, ultimately free. She is simply freedom embodied.

I put the journal down. Having only really just met Dan, there's no way I would've picked her for a dominant Freedom Cup. Why on earth doesn't she leave her shop? I suddenly feel ashamed for reading the journal.

Instead of anger at her rejection, a sense of pity takes its place. Sure, Dan's actions can be perceived as rude, but there's something behind the behaviour. She's trying to fill a Cup when she behaves the way she does. Instead of being upset with her, or anyone for that matter, I should only be upset with the behaviour they are choosing to fill their Cups, and not take it personally.

The smell of beer soaking into the carpet wafts around the room and, as dank as it is, I feel the urge to have a drink rise inside of me. Wait. What is it, this urge? Where has it come from? Sandi said that Dr Glasser believed every behaviour is to fill a need. What need, or Cup, am I trying to fill?

The smell of the beer starts to burn in my veins and I have to decide whether to go get a drink or get out of this room. I decide to go for a walk.

Outside on the street, the ground is littered with brown and golden leaves. To get the smell of beer out of my nostrils, I inhale the air deep into my lungs. I do this several times, and instantly feel a calm come over me. I close my eyes and continue to breathe through my nose. I am suddenly overcome by an intoxicating perfume. It almost weakens me at my knees, and as phantom-like as it came, so too does it disappear. Soon, another scent arrives. This time it is a pungent smell – the strong smell of nail polish. But it, too, disappears after only a moment. Almost as soon as I notice it's gone, does the sweet aroma of pastry arrive. What's happening? Have these scents always been there? Had I previously just dismissed them? Perhaps I've been ignoring them so that I could carry on more efficiently with my day. This must be what they mean by 'stopping to smell the roses'. I wonder what other senses are more heightened if I truly tune into them?

Listening in, I am suddenly aware of the nearby traffic. I can hear the engines, differentiating them from car, truck and motorcycle. Horns. What else can I hear? Children. There are children nearby. In fact, it's children's laughter. Deeper still, it's unabridged laughter I can hear. No, wait. What I am hearing in their laughter is pure joy. I can hear Fun Cups being filled… Wait, what is that now. Birds. My god, how glorious are those bird songs?

I find myself strolling, listening, smelling, looking. I watch a caterpillar walk along a stone fence. It's fuzzy, almost humorous. I focus on the mildew on the stone; deep and shallow shades of green, filled with microscopic life. Remarkable. Has the world always been this marvellous? Only half an hour ago I was wallowing in self-pity. Now I see the world is so much larger than myself, and I find that so wonderful.

I reach for my flask, and realise as I do so, that it's from habit. Maybe I am just a foolish old man but I know I drink to escape – to fulfil a part in life that I've almost forgotten I have been playing – and out of habit. I've made drinking a normality. But right now, I can see that it would only stop all this. This, right now, using all my senses, is filling my Cups. Right now, I don't need a drink. I spend the next hour just wandering around my small neighbourhood smelling, watching, touching, looking.

That evening I eat at the local Indian restaurant. I experiment with different dishes that I'd never thought of trying. With each new dish I close my eyes and take in all the aromas and tastes. I listen to the restaurant's soundtrack which I must've filtered out before. Most importantly, I only have two drinks with dinner.

When I get home I try calling Darlene, I feel certain she would be pleased to hear the sobriety in my voice. But, when I call, there's still no dial tone. I have only two more drinks before getting into bed. I open the journal again, this time to the very last page.

Dan flew into a rage today. The afternoon started fine. We were picnicking, and I was using the strawberries to flirtatiously rub around her neck. We kissed so passionately that it felt like we were courting again. As soon as I brought up the wedding she was dismissive. When I pressed her, asking if perhaps she really didn't want to marry me, she could only laugh. Instead of assuring me with words, she kissed my cheek. I pressed her again letting her know how vulnerable I was feeling, only then did she say that she was pleased about marrying me. She said that to her it was just a ceremony. She doesn't need anyone outside of us to secure this bond. No god, no government, and certainly no family. All she needs is me. I said although she didn't need to invite her family, I would like it if she would at least tell them about me. That she does plan to spend the rest of her life with me. That is when she upturned the strawberry punnet and knocked over the sparkling. With a finger in my face she told me that if I ever try to reach out to her family then we're through.

What on earth could have happened between Dan and her parents?

Before long I feel the euphoric paralysis of sleep begin to creep over me. It comes upon me so warm and embracive, like a caring mother holding me to her breast. So long had the drink taken me into the void that I'd almost forgotten how wonderful falling asleep can be.

My sleep is disrupted by my phone ringing beside my bed. I sit up, feeling disoriented. When I gather my bearings, I reach for my phone.

'Hello,' I say.

'Frank?' comes a woman's voice, 'You won't believe what I've discovered.'

'Darlene?' I ask, rubbing my eyes.

'No, it's Dan. Frank, listen to me. You need to wake up, I need to tell you about something I uncovered. I was researching Schopenhauer further, using the wonderous beast that is the internet, and I came across the philosopher Friedrich Nietzsche.'

I pull the phone away from my ear to look at the time. 'It's 3:20am,' I say.

'What I didn't know,' Dan continues, 'was that he was heavily influenced by Schopenhauer and his idea of the Will to Life, which we discussed. The more he thought upon it, however, he started to believe that this irrational, unconscious force within all things was actually a Will to Power. Nietzsche believed all things desire domination over other things, themselves or their environment. Not necessarily in grand domineering ways, such as political and military power, but sometimes as simple as pursuing a goal, whether we are conscious of it or not. Even as far as self-overcoming, as he liked to put it. What I really want to tell you about, however, is something that has come to me tonight while thinking upon Schopenhauer's Will to Life, and now Nietzsche's Will to Power. Are you ready for it, Frank… Frank?'

'Yes, I'm here,' I say, listening with my eyes closed.

'Okay, brace yourself Frank. Get this… It's the Will to Fill... Schopenhauer said Will to Life, Nietzsche said Will to Power, these are just two basic human life needs being met; the Safety Cup, and its drive for security, and the Mastery Cup and its drive for self-competence. Frank, there are three more Wills. The Will to Fun and Learning, and its drive for joy, the Will to Freedom, and it's drive for autonomy, and the Will to Connection, and its drive for self-worth. Whatever your dominant Cup is, nay, which ever Cup is requiring filling at that moment, because even our smallest Cups require filling, that is where the Will to Fill arises, and fills that need first. This is why sometimes we see these other Wills fall short. If our Connection Cup is empty we may be driven to undertake behaviours that may put the Will to Mastery aside. If our Freedom Cup is empty we may be driven to undertake behaviours that may put the Will to Safety aside, and so forth.'

Dan must have sensed that I am vaguely following. I understand what she means but am a little lost by the philosophical terminology, and perhaps by the abrupt awakening.

'Essentially, there is an unconscious Will behind each Cup that drives us to fill that Cup when it is emptying. Our dominant Cups just require more, so we usually see those behaviours more often. However, whichever Cup is emptying at that moment is where the Will to Fill will arrive first… What I am thinking with all this is we don't have to be at the mercy of our Cups. We can look at filling them in ways that are more life affirming. We can choose to fill them in ways that are satisfying to us, and not just us satisfying the Will to Fill. You could say it takes us from an observer of life to a participant. Now, that sounds far more rewarding and meaningful. I will discuss this further when you come in tomorrow. Okay, see you then. Come in around four-thirty,' Dan says, and abruptly hangs up the phone.

JACK

7. YESTERDAY'S PAIN

The nurse comes back into my room, sends me a sympathetic smile, and adjusts my father's pillow. I can't help but wonder if nursing and other caring professions generally appeal to those with dominant Connection Cups? As I sit there and ponder this thought, I think back to the time when I was twelve and had broken my wrist. I attempted to skateboard down a concrete half-pipe, twice the size of any I had ever skated on. Even before hearing Frank's tale, I know what willed me to attempt it: my pubescent Will to Life had me trying to impress Amanda Stevens. Now that's a name I haven't thought of in a long time. I can still picture her there with her mousy brown hair, knobbly knees, and her mouth full of braces. She was wearing a Robert Smith T-shirt and I was infatuated. To this day I still think I could have made it, but the moment I dropped in, I looked up at her and saw she was watching Kenny Dawkins skate. I lost my concentration, ended up landing on my arm – my skateboard, humiliatingly, rolled on to her feet, hitting her in the shins. The pain in my wrist was electric, and as much as I tried to maintain a straight, cool face in front of everyone, my eyes wouldn't stop tearing. I didn't let out my first wail of pain until after I skated away from the park and was down the street. By the time I got home, my arm was in agony. I found my mother sitting outside the front door, still in her dressing gown, smoking a cigarette.

'What's wrong with you?' she asked.

'I think I broke my arm.'

'You did not. You're just a bloody sook,' she said.

'No mum, really, I need you to take me to the hospital,' I pleaded. My mother eyed me suspiciously. She didn't want to have to get out of her dressing gown, I assumed. When we got to the hospital, the burly triage nurse looked at me as if she was just as inconvenienced as my mother. She certainly didn't have a dominant Connection Cup. The nurse that attended me, however, was much more comforting. Even, tenderly caressing my forehead with her thumb when asking me what had happened. It felt foreign, yet so very soothing. I remember melting into that tenderness. My mother must have been able to sense my warming to the affection.

'He's just a bloody sook,' she said.

I'm brought back to the room and to this moment when it looks like my father takes a deeper breath. When I look closer it seems just as shallow as before. Perhaps I imagined it.

'You don't talk much do you?' Frank calls out.

'I was taught never say anything that doesn't improve on silence,' I reply. The speed and callousness of my words surprise even me, and I'm unsure why I said them. I know I didn't mean it. As much as I hate to admit it, I am intrigued by this man's Cups fable. The silence that befalls us is nearly as long as the one at the beginning of the night.

'It sounds like you care deeply for your daughter,' I eventually sigh.

Another silence.

Frank mumbles something incoherent and then says, 'Okay.' But not to me. 'It wasn't until I got really sick that Darlene came to visit me, hey sweetheart?' he says. 'I guess it's the same with you and your father.'

'What did you just say?'

'We all have our reasons,' he says.

I shake my head to myself. 'You know,' I say, and point my left hand at my father, even though Frank can't see it through the curtain. 'He didn't even reach out to us to tell us he was sick. It was the hospital who contacted my brother.'

'So why did you come?' Frank asks.

That's a good question. Why am I here? Why, after all these years, have I come to see a man who cares nothing about me? I exhale deeply through my nose and lower my head.

'… Maybe to tell him things.'

'What kind of things?'

'… I don't know. Perhaps ask him why he was the way he was?'

'And how is that?' Frank presses.

Frank's honest and curt questions somehow make me want to speak my thoughts aloud. Perhaps it's because Frank has been doing all the talking tonight. Maybe it's because I want to articulate it to myself.

'It's strange, but I want answers. Yet part of me waited until I knew he wasn't able to give them… Maybe I'm afraid of the answers I might get.'

'What kind of answers scare you, son?'

'That maybe he really didn't care. That maybe he really never did love me. I don't know.' I shake my head and I look into my open hands. 'Maybe I just want to know why he didn't want me… I was just a little boy and he didn't want me… He didn't want me when I needed him the most.'

I feel my abdomen tense. 'Where was he when I was crying myself to sleep every night?' I look up from my hands to my father's ashen face. 'Where was he when I was getting chased home from school?'

My chest now starts to tense. 'Where was he when all the other kids were playing with brand new toys and I had to wear my brother's hand-me downs?'

My right-hand turns into a fist. 'Where was he when all the other fathers took their kids to football? Where was he when my brother had to make us lunch and take us to school? Where was he when Mum would go out all night and I'd stay awake in fear until she got home?'

My right arm is quivering against the fist. 'Where was he when social services came? Where was he when I was having a child of my own?'

I look down at my hand. I release it and it turns from white back to pink.

I look back at his face and say, 'It's because of you I find it hard to trust people. It's because of you I stayed in an unhealthy relationship for so damn long, terrified she would take her love away from me. It's because of you I'm so angry all the time but too afraid to show it. It's because of you I find it so goddam hard to love myself... I was just a little boy, Dad. I was just a little boy who needed you. I needed you and you weren't there... I just wanted to hear you say that you loved me. I just wanted to hear you say that you were sorry...'

Something wet rolls down my right cheek, and my eyes blur. I exhale deeply through my nose again. For weeks I told myself I wouldn't come up here. Then, when I arrived here tonight, I told myself I would only be here for a moment. Now that I have been here for a couple of hours, I'm starting to question my own behaviour. What Cup, or Cups, are motivating me to stay?

I turn my voice to Frank, 'I guess I waited until he was no longer conscious because I'm afraid he wouldn't feel any of those things.'

'To hold onto old pain, son, is to hold onto yesterday. Yesterday no longer exists, what's hurting you is only the memory of that pain. You're not a little boy anymore. Don't let yesterday empty today's Cups.'

FRANK

8. THE CONNECTION CUP

On the train the next afternoon on my way to Dan's store, I think about my failed marriage. Where did it all start to go wrong? Surely it wasn't always bad? I remember once when we were newly coupled, as I lay in bed and she got up to get ready for the day, I heard the shudder of the pipes, and the sounds of the shower door open. I leapt out of bed, rushed out the front door, and flew down the two flights of stairs of our unit complex. I hurried barefoot through the cold concrete carpark until I reached the communal backyard, where a giant frangipani tree stood. I searched the tree looking for her most perfect flower. Every time I thought I'd found it, I'd see a smidge of brown at the end of at least one of the yellow and pink petals. Then I saw it. It was at eye level and arm's length in. I snapped it off a few inches down the stem and raced back up the stairs. When I reached the front door, I rubbed the light sweat from my forehead into my black hair. As I headed back into the bedroom I heard the shower turn off. I ducked under the covers over my side of the bed, and carefully arranged the flower on her pillow. I closed my eyes feigning sleep and heard the bedroom door open.

'Oh, Frank,' I heard her say. 'You're so sweet.' And with my eyes still closed, I couldn't hold back my smile. So, where did it all start to go wrong?

When I get to Dan's store, she's buzzing around her shop. There are no customers but she's moving with a sense of purpose.

'Hey Frank,' she says when she sees me. 'I'm sorry about the way I acted the other day. I am also sorry for calling you in the early hours.'

'You have nothing to apologise for,' I reply, somewhat confused by her geniality. It's foreign to what I've experienced with her so far.

'I've been thinking,' she says, with her back to me, leading me to the room again, 'that we should tackle the Connection Cup today, in the same way we did with the Safety Cup. Let's again look at characteristics and behaviours and find some examples of people who we think would identify as having a dominant Connection Cup. Sound good?'

'Sure,' I say as she opens the door.

'Can I get you a tea?'

'No, thank you,' I reply, as I sit down.

Dan turns on the kettle and pulls down two mugs from the shelf. 'So, I was thinking today of the behaviours of those I now recognise as having a dominant Connection Cup,' she says. 'Although not always, generally they seem to be very sociable people. It might just be those with dominant Connection Cups and big Fun Cups, but I see them as sociable, empathetic, and generous. What comes to mind when you think of those with a dominant Connection Cup, Frank?'

Dan pours the boiling water into the two mugs with the tea infusers inside them.

'Well,' I say, 'what comes to mind for me are words like friendship, belonging, love, acceptance. What else?... I guess also sharing and cooperation, respect, bonding. Affection, even.'

I am surprised at how easily the words seem to flow out of me today compared to when we discussed the Safety Cup.

'So, we could say someone who has a dominant Connection Cup may have a stronger desire to be connected with others, and are often empathetic, caring, and generous,' Dan says, as she places a mug of tea in front of me. 'Do you think they might also be moved easily by certain experiences others may regard as trivial? For instance, I remember giving a customer a free tote bag once and her eyes welled as though I had given her my shop.'

'Yeah, that makes sense.'

'You know I read a book a few years ago, well, half read it. Love Languages, I believe it was called. The gist of it, though, was that we each project and interpret love and connection in different ways. For instance, one person may prefer to use words. Therefore, they may fill their Connection Cup by telling their partners, or friends and family, how much they care about them. There are also those who prefer to do things for others, like helping out. We could also see this as Connection Cup filling. What else was there? That's right, another one is giving presents and other gifts. I can remember a friend in school who I now realise had a dominant Connection Cup. She never missed my birthday and always bought me something, even though I never bought her a gift. Now, I know there are two more in this theory… oh yes, spending uninterrupted time with someone. Quality time, that was it. And I believe the final one was something about always wanting to touch, as in hugging, and things like that. That one is my worst nightmare, and I have so many customers who always want to hug me. Urgh. So, we can see someone with a dominant Connection Cup may fill their Cup by behaving in any of those ways.'

I nod, impressed.

'Hey, do you know anything about flow-state?' Dan asks. 'On your paper was a name I had to look up – a name I certainly can't pronounce. Chic-sent, chicszen-me… Csikszentmihalyi. Something like that. Here look,' she says pointing to the name on the paper. 'Anyway, I researched him and he speaks of this flow-state, which he said is when we feel and perform at our best. He said that when we are in flow, we are completely involved in whatever activity it is for its own sake. That is, our ego is essentially forgotten in that moment. As a side effect, time seems to fly by unnoticed. I have a hunch that the man wrote this name down on your piece of paper because flow-state must have something to do with Cup Filling. I think, though I'm not one hundred percent sure yet, that whatever activity we usually experience flow in may be aligned with our more dominant Cups. So, for instance, those with a dominant Connection Cup may experience flow when they are amongst friends and family. Their flow activity is filling their dominant Cup. Do you see what I mean? Just as a person with a dominant Freedom Cup may experience flow when they're travelling, or maybe doing something creative. Those with a dominant Mastery Cup may experience it working on a task. They're in the moment, and time has flown by, while filling their Cups.'

I can't help but think back to my visits with my daughter after my divorce, and how the hours flew by like minutes. I was experiencing flow filling my Connection Cup with Darlene, only to have it emptied once more when it was time to go. How she used to weep and cling to my leg when it was time to leave. Then, as the years passed, she became colder towards me. She started to associate me with her pain. She started to say things that suggested that I was the reason I didn't live with her and her mum anymore, that it was me who chose to end the marriage and leave the family. I didn't have the heart to tell her that it was all taken away from me. As much of a relief it would've been for me to tell her the truth, it would've hurt her. So, I carried the heartache so she didn't have to.

'You know, come to think of it,' Dan says, 'I used to have a customer who said not long after he'd leave his house he'd receive a message from his wife saying how much she loved him and missed him already. He was confused, in his mind he had only just been with her. His Connection Cup was much smaller and therefore was filled enough by the time they parted to stay full enough until they were back together. Her Connection Cup was much larger and required more to fill it, hence the messages of love, her larger social circle, and her overall caring nature and empathy.'

'Okay,' I say, 'we've got a fair idea of what someone with a dominant Connection Cup may look like. What about someone with a small Connection Cup? Do you think then that a person with a small Connection Cup may, at times, be perceived as callous with their filling of their other dominant Cups? As in, they don't realise that their behaviours could affect other people's Connection Cups, because they would not be affected by it if they were on the receiving end of the behaviour?'

'That makes sense,' Dan says. 'Actually, a person with a dominant Connection Cup may even appear clingy or oversensitive to others whose Connection Cup isn't as big. I think that their need for love and belonging may also have them easily hurt? For example, if a loving act is not reciprocated. The funny thing is that I have to admit I don't have the biggest Connection Cup, as you may have guessed. However, when I was younger I used to require the love and belonging of others. I craved it. Now that I am much older I don't seem to need it anymore. Is it possible that our Cup sizes are not static, and they can change size?'

I ponder this for a moment. 'Well Sandi said our Cup sizes are genetic, and do not change. What changes is how full or empty they are and how you fill them. I think it is entirely possible that you used to require love and connection from others, however, as you got older, and of course wiser, you realised that perhaps you didn't need their acceptance. I don't think your Connection Cup changed size, I think you just learned how to fill it with self-love. It was your behavioural choice that changed, and therefore how full the Cup is, not the size of your Cup.'

A lightbulb-smile filters across her face, 'That makes perfect sense. Thank you, Frank. Growing up I had low self-esteem. I felt powerless and unloved. I constantly needed the approval and recognition of others. However, the more competent I became – which fits more with the Mastery Cup – the more I was able to admire myself. I think my growing self-esteem led to a lot more self-love.'

I sip my tea, as we both ponder in silence.

'So,' I say, but then realise that I don't know how to articulate my thoughts, so I stop. 'Okay,' I try again. 'Why do we even have this Connection Cup? We know every behaviour is to satisfy a need, or to fill a Cup, but what is the function behind the need? Why do some of us have a larger Connection Cup than others, and why are we driven to fill it? Essentially, what is the Will to Fill in relation to the Connection Cup?'

'I was just pondering this too,' Dan beams. 'I think, possibly, it could also come back to the Will to Life. The Connection Cup could be tied to the Safety Cup. You see the Connection Cup represents the need for love, belonging and acceptance. As human beings we are social creatures. We live together in communities and we connect to one another. So much so, our very survival depends on it. We need others to survive and reproduce. Therefore, the Connection Cup, which we think is selfless, actually may have a level of selfishness to fulfil our own needs. Needs for safety, security, and reproduction. Hmmm, this doesn't feel so romantic anymore if it's biological and sociological. Does that make us all egotistical, that we only love to ensure our safety and reproduction?'

Dismayed, I say, 'Wait, what about those stories when people place themselves at risk to save others they care about?'

'Maybe that's still the Will to Life, but the empathy level of the Connection Cup is so large it's looking after the survival of the offspring, or even community. Perhaps those with a dominant Connection Cup and small

Safety Cup could be more sacrificial – more empathetic. Come to think of it, Socrates died for others. My husband told me that he died so that we could think. He was given the option to save himself when on trial but chose the greater good of humankind. Clearly, he had a dominant Connection Cup and a small Safety Cup. The difference between Socrates accepting the death penalty for the sake of his fellow man, and a mother throwing herself in front of a car to save her child, is that Socrates' action took cognition where the mother's action was reactive – an instinctual sacrifice.'

Although I don't know the story of Socrates and how he met his end, I don't need to in order to understand Dan's point.

'I don't mean to be gloomy,' I say, 'but what about suicide? Here we see so many with an empty Connection Cup choosing to override the Will to Life, or Safety Cup, and take their own life.'

Dan's mouth tightens for a moment.

'Actually,' I continue, 'that could even fit with the other Cups too. If someone feels completely powerless, one power they may have is the choice to end their own life. Or perhaps even with an empty Freedom Cup. They are free to make that devastating choice… Come to think of it, how terrible that we see that so often in detention centres.'

Dan falters again, and it looks as though the colour is draining from her face. After a moment she regains her composure and says, 'I guess empty Cups, other than the Safety Cup that is, can make us choose behaviours that override the Will to Life… Wait!'

Dan jumps out of her seat and into her shop. She returns moments later with three new books.

'I'm surprised no one has interrupted us today,' I say.

Dan flicks through one of the volumes in her hands and, as her eyes search the pages, says, 'I closed the shop so no one could come in.'

She reads the page, then flicks ahead several more and keeps reading. I can't help but wonder if Dan's the only person I've ever met who doesn't feel awkward silences. While Dan reads, I begin to muse. I remember when Darlene was two and would wait for me to get home from work. As soon as I would walk in the door, she would take me by the hand and into her room. Amongst all her store-bought toys, what she loved the most was a large cardboard box I had fashioned into a small house for her. I cut open a door, and some windows into it. Inside she had her favourite teddy bears and some other treasures. She'd make me squeeze into this little house with her and pour me some imaginary tea. As I ponder this memory, melancholy touches my heart.

'Everything was fine with my daughter, well, so I thought. I really thought things were on the mend with our relationship. Of course, she stayed away if I'd been drinking…' My accidental confession to my alcoholism forces me to drop my gaze, '…but otherwise things were going well enough. And then the moment she had her baby she stopped returning my calls and refused to see me… I haven't seen or spoken to her since. It's been nearly six years.'

Dan stops reading. 'I'm sorry to hear that, Frank.'

'I remember a dream I had about six months after losing my family. I was living on a friend's couch with nothing but a suitcase of clothes, while my wife, Jane, was travelling around Europe with her new man. In the dream I walked into my old house – it must've been morning because the sun was rising – and I went to check on Darlene who was still asleep in her bed. I walked into the main bedroom and saw Jane lying under the covers on her side. I walked around the bed and climbed in behind her pulling the covers over us. I shuffled my way towards her so that her back was pressed against my front and my arm was wrapped around her. Our bodies together, warm, I was relaxed. For the first time in months all my pain ebbed away, and I let myself fall into the moment. My mind was clear and empty and I timed my breathing so that it matched Jane's. We were one living being. I felt whole again, lying there. In that moment I still had a daughter, I still had a wife, a family, a bedroom, a home. I still had a life and I was happy. I remember this contentment like I've never felt before or since. I felt fulfilled.

'After a minute, however, a consciousness seemed to tap me on the shoulder and say "That's enough now, it's time to go. This is no longer real. You do not have this anymore". I remember wanting to hold tighter, to not let go. I felt my chest quiver and convulse and tried to steady myself so I didn't disturb Jane. I began to cry and pull my arm away from Jane so as not to wake her. I felt her hand reach behind her, take my wrist and pull it back around her. I was crying but Jane said nothing, she just held my hand tightly. A voice then seemed to echo in my ear from the waking world which said, "It's time to go now", and then I woke up…

'It's not that we had small Connection Cups. Both of us have dominant Connection Cups. Perhaps we just didn't communicate well enough to each other. We spoke a lot, but nothing was ever said. Perhaps we expected too much of each other instead of taking ownership of our needs… I don't know.'

'How long ago did you say you were married?'

'Nearly thirty years ago. I haven't been in a relationship since then.'

'Why not?'

'I guess part of me feels unworthy. For some reason I carry the guilt as though it were entirely my fault she left. Another part is fear. What if it happens again?'

Dan's eyebrows push upwards and she reaches out and takes hold of the back of my hand. 'I guess to love is to be vulnerable. So, you could either lock your heart away where it will be safe but grow hard and lonely, or you can take a chance on love again. Perhaps the risk of heartbreak is worth more than the suffering of loneliness.'

Ashamedly, I hadn't thought Dan capable of such tenderness. I feign a smile, 'I guess the only thing to do in the face of life's suffering is to laugh at it and keep moving forward.'

'Sometimes I think we just have unrealistic expectations of love,' Dan says. 'This can cause us so much pain and can be Cup emptying. We watch movies, we read literature, we listen to music, all of which portray romantic love as something ethereal. Even family love. Real love is disagreeing from time to time. Real love is forgetting the washing is in the washing machine. Real love is fighting with your children but still doing everything in your power to keep them safe. Dare I say, real love is farting in bed.' Dan holds up a book... 'I've only just started looking through this, but the author, Alain De Botton, says that love is not an indescribable feeling, but a skill. A skill we could also apply to self-love, I guess. We can also do our best at understanding love too, by demystifying it by looking at its different types. There is passionate or sexual love. There's Platonic love - which is friendship. There's the kind of love you have for your family. Universal love, which you have for your fellow humans. I guess, when we look at it that way, the Connection Cup is certainly about belonging. It always seems to incorporate more than just the self, so I suppose it's not that selfish at all... Looking back on it, my husband had a large Connection Cup. Oh, the things we would fight about. Isn't it funny that we think that a lover's bond should automatically turn us all into mind readers? We get upset because our loved one doesn't know why we're upset, and then we get even more upset thinking that if they don't know why, then possibly they are not really the one for us. How dumb we are sometimes... I really miss that stubborn bastard.'

I watch Dan slip into nostalgia. After a few moments I see she needs some time to herself. 'How about we call it a day?' I suggest and send her my most comforting smile. When she looks up I can see her eyes are glazed, but she smiles and nods.

JACK

9. CUP-FILLING MISCHIEF

'How long ago was all this?' I ask Frank.

Beep.

'Jesus, you scared the hell out of me. I forgot you were there. I don't know, a year ago? Five years ago, maybe? I'm not sure anymore. Some things just confuse me these days, you know? Simple things. Words even. Sometimes the world just doesn't seem to make sense for a few short moments. I've heard them say dementia. It's not dementia. I just get confused sometimes, that's all. Just confused.'

Beep.

Beep.

Beep.

'You know one memory I have growing up with my brother,' I say to Frank, 'is the time we were visiting my father, and he allowed us to go to the shopping centre alone. I think it was the last year my brother came down to visit Dad with me, so I must've been around eight at the time. I remember we went into a department store and were looking through the cassette tapes and CDs. My brother found the new Meat Loaf album. Even if we combined our money we wouldn't have enough to buy it. My brother held up the CD and the cassette tape side by side. I thought he was just enthralled by the art on the cover until I realised what he was doing. He was measuring them. "Come here," he said, when I stood by his side, he shoved the cassette in my pocket. My heart pounded as we left the store. I was sure everyone was watching us. When we'd gotten around the corner into the food court my brother smiled at me. We had gotten away with it. Our celebration, however, was too soon. A giant of a man put his hand on my shoulder. "You boys better come with me," he said, and he took us into a back room of the department store. For the next half an hour he grilled us on our theft and was wondering what to do to us. Then he came up with a solution. He got all our details and said that he would be sending the police around to talk to our father. Since we were cooperative, he told us that to ease the damage he would give us a head start home first to confess before the police arrived.

'When we got home and told Dad what had happened, he was furious. I'd never seen him so animated. It was beyond anger. It was disappointment. The police never came – the man at the store had tricked us into confessing to Dad and have him punish us.

'Thinking on that day now, two things come to mind. Firstly, I suppose if my father really was indifferent to my brother and I, then he wouldn't have gotten that mad. And secondly, we got busted for Meat Loaf.'

Frank lets out a dry wheeze of a laugh.

'That reminds me of the time when I was about sixteen, and hanging out with my best friend James,' Frank says. 'We were drinking Southern Comfort and wandering the streets, looking for other cool kids, as we did in the day. As we wandered, beyond tipsy, we saw the hotel that had a new wing being built. They'd been working on this for a year and it looked nearly ready. The rest of the hotel had remained open, so we carefully snuck our way inside trying our best not to be seen by the concierge. We found our way to the new wing. It looked beautiful. Fresh. These were the days before those key-card entry things, where people still needed real keys to open and lock doors. Anyway, my friend and I pulled down on one of the door handles and it opened. The room was immaculate. Never before had anyone stayed there. She was a beauty. First thing we did was raid the mini bar. We ate all the chocolates and then drank the beer and small bottles of spirits. When we finished everything in the room, we went out and tried the next room. Success again. It too was unlocked. Once more we raided the confectionaries and drinks. By now, we were well liquored-up. Once we finished everything in this room, we tried the next room. Would you believe, it was also unlocked? I went straight for the bar fridge while my friend went to use the bathroom. As he opened the door a voice boomed "What are you doing in here?" James bolted past me and out of the room. Behind him a naked man came stumbling after him with his pants around his ankles. He must have walked in on him on the toilet. By the time the man got to the door he kicked his pants off and stood completely bare looking out into the hall for my friend. It was all happening so fast and was so surreal, I felt like I was watching a movie. It was then that I realised I was trapped. Right on cue, the man turned and looked at me. An icy hand gripped my heart. He came at me. I jumped over the bed, and when I turned, I saw he was doing the same. I looked at the door and made a run for it. He grabbed onto my jacket, but I was able to fling his hand away. I sprinted out and into the hallway and ran at full speed until I turned a corner into the next wing. I was about to ease my step when I realised the naked man was still behind me. He had continued to chase me in the nude.

'Adrenalin coursed through my legs as I picked up my speed again. I looked up in the distance and I could see James. While the look on my face must've been sheer panic, he had the most amused expression I've ever seen. He turned around much like a relay runner might and waited for me to reach him, before we both ran back into the foyer and then out into the night. When we finally found a place to stop and catch our breath, we burst into laughter. It was that once-in-a-lifetime kind of laughter of both relief and hilarity.'

I couldn't contain my own laughter at Frank's story, or how alive his voice was while telling it. It was as though recounting that gave him back ten years.

Beep.

'You could say that that night filled your Fun Cup,' I say.

'I think it nearly filled all my Cups, young man,' Frank chuckled.

'My name's Jack.'

'Well I'm pleased to meet you, young Jack.'

Another silence overcomes us. I look at my father, and for the first time tonight he's starting to look more like a human to me. How different his behaviours were to my own. For the past twenty years I'd seen him as a kind of villain. This person I believed to be cold and indifferent to his children. A person who seemed to care more about his own damn mediocrity than the love of his family. If every behaviour is simply to satisfy a need, or fill a Cup, is it possible that his Cups Profile is just so different to mine that it caused us to misunderstand each other? Is it possible he just has a very small Connection Cup, which only takes a drop to fill? Could he simply not understand the love and connection I needed growing up? This does not excuse his behaviours but does help me to understand them.

'So, Frank,' I say. 'What's the next Cup?'

Beep.

'Frank?'

Beep.

'… Frank?'

'Hold on, damnit… Okay, where were we? Oh yeah, the next Cup is the Mastery Cup.'

FRANK

10. UNTIL IT SLEEPS

On my way to Dan's shop the next morning I stop to watch a street performer in the mall. What's peculiar about this man is that although he has ripped jeans, a black faded T-shirt with some obscene looking creature on it, long greasy hair, and a face full of piercings, he has his violin case open and is playing Wagner. I watch him as I sip at my flask. The violin doesn't look like an instrument, but an extension of him. He moves with it as though it's another limb. Although I can hear an extremely talented young man, what I see are the hours and dedication it has taken for him to master his craft, and in a sense, his own world. In fact, it is more than his own world. It looks like it transcends even him. It is as though he is an extension of the music being played; a vehicle in which he and the violin melds together. He isn't cognisant of his hands playing, he and the violin are merely a manifestation of the music. In essence, he doesn't try to play the music, his hours of mastery have him become the music.

It's midday when I arrive at Dan's shop, it's the earliest I've ever been here, but the store is locked. There's no 'Closed' sign up either, or any indication of how long it will be closed for.

I go to get some lunch at a nearby café, and when I return to the shop an hour later the door's still impenetrable. I peer through the window and see only darkness. Didn't she say that she doesn't go outside?

I leave again and find a department store where I buy a notebook and a pen, and find my way to a café in an alfresco piazza. I order a cappuccino and a croissant, and sit back, watching the world around me. As the pigeons coo, the maître d' fusses, and cutlery clinks, I see Cups in others nearly as clearly as I imagined I would be able to if they wore a sign above their head that showed their Cups Profile. I watch a woman interrogating a man at a nearby table – on what looks like a first date – demanding to know his opinion on some personal dilemma. His replies are calm but his body language betrays him, as he leans away from the woman. Her Mastery Cup is trying to control the conversation, but his dominant Freedom Cup would likely have him not return her calls once this date is over.

At another table, a man keeps his eyes on his hand that is fussing with his glass, while he continuously talks about his health. His companion leans in expectantly, and rarely blinks as she's absorbed by his face. His dominant Cup is Safety, hers is Connection.

I play this game all afternoon. I notice it's not so much the words spoken but the totality of the behaviours. Micro behaviours, perhaps undetectable were I forced to give explanations, but using that innate part of us we sometimes mistakenly refer to as gut-feeling, when it is just the entirety of our unconscious analysis.

When I return to Dan's bookstore I find that it's still closed. An unease creeps into my belly. I can't tell if it's fear, that perhaps she's had an accident; anger, that perhaps she's decided to shut me out and research the rest alone; or rejection, that she just doesn't like me? Either way, it feels awful. I cross the street and wander around until I find a bar that's attached to the bottom of a hotel. The woman behind the bar must be in her early thirties, she's wearing a white buttoned shirt and a bowtie. She resembles Darlene.

'Can I help you, sir?' she asks.

'Whiskey neat, please.'

It takes only a moment until it hits the back of my throat, and I order another. How could Dan do this to me? But, did she do this to me? What if I am reading into something that isn't there? What if she's had an accident? But what if she just can't stand me? Would that be so impossible to believe? My father couldn't stand me. My ex-wife couldn't stand me. Hell, it even seems Darlene can't stand me. Why would I be so surprised if Dan feels the same way?

'Another, please,' I ask.

I run my fingers along the mahogany bar, feeling all the varnished cracks and crevices. I become aware of the music. Wagner again. This time through the sound system. What a strange coincidence.

'You know, you look just like my daughter,' I say to the lady behind the bar. She gives me an awkward, unimpressed smile.

'Oh, no. Don't get me wrong,' I continue, 'I'm not a creepy old man. You just look a lot like her. She's very beautiful too.'

She shakes her head and turns her back to me. I was being earnest and she still thinks that I was hitting on her. Well, to hell with her. And to hell with Dan too.

'Another, if it's not too much trouble,' I ask again.

After one more drink, I fumble with my phone to try Darlene's number. Again, no dial tone. You know what? To hell with you, too, Darlene… No, no I didn't mean that.

'Another,' I say, raising my glass toward the girl.

I'm suddenly aware of some young businessmen in suits laughing obnoxiously. Their smugness, their elitism, their goddamn exuberance gets to me. 'Will you guys show some respect for your environment?' I bark. Either they don't hear me, or they purposely ignore me.

'Bourbon, please.'

How on earth did I get here? I had a wife, a home, a family. Man, I had it all. Now it's all gone, and here I am; old, alone, and pathetic. I become aware of the businessmen now talking to the girl behind the bar.

'Hey you bloody punks. Do you think I'm impressed that you have those suits on? Do you think she's impressed?' I point to the girl. 'No, we're not. So, why don't you get lost.'

The men look confused. One says something back to me, but I can't understand it. Then they laugh. One tries to pat me on the shoulder condescendingly, but I shove him away.

'You don't have to put up with this Darlene,' I say. 'Wait… whatever your name is.'

The girl and the suits look at me like I am speaking some other language. From behind me a giant of man puts his hand on my shoulder. He points to the door and says something incoherent to me.

'To hell with all of you,' I say, in my confused state. I stumble onto the street. I'm confused because the road is wet now, and steam rises from the pores of the asphalt. I don't need anybody. I raised myself when my father left. I've looked after myself since my wife left. I don't need anyone.

I look up and see Dan's store. I stumble over and start banging on the glass. 'Hey, open up. Open up!' I call out.

I do this over and over until I see a shadowy figure. 'Hey, open up!' The figure just stands there as I continue to bang and yell. I do this over and over until I tire, and collapse against the door and slide to the ground. I must've dozed off and when I come to, I become aware of flashing blue and red lights. Two men in uniform and thick belts come over to talk to me. I don't know exactly what they're saying, but soon I am in the back of their car. I either black out or fall asleep, because my next memory is them helping me open my front door. Hours later I am holding the toilet bowl as I weep.

FRANK

11. THE MASTERY CUP

I stay away from Dan's bookstore for the next three next days. How on earth am I going to be able to apologise for this? Even if she accepts my apology, I am so embarrassed for my behaviour that I'm not sure I want to face her.

When I summon up the courage and arrive at her store just after lunch, it's closed again. What if she did have an accident days ago and I've waited this long? Wait, didn't I see her inside the shop the night the police arrived? Maybe I imagined that I saw her there, I wasn't really in a state to trust my senses. I pull my phone out of my pocket and look for her number. Still standing outside her locked door, I call her. After several rings a recorded voice on the other end asks me to leave a message. I hang up and put my phone away.

Cupping my hands around the sides of my eyes, I peer into the dark shop. It looks as though there might be a light on out the back, perhaps it's coming from the room we were studying in. Was that movement I saw? I dial the number again. After six or seven rings, Dan answers the phone.

'Frank. I can't talk to you right now,' she says.

'I… I really just want to know you are okay… I just want to say…'

'Frank. I have to go,' she says and hangs up.

My stomach turns. I start to pace, but my frail knees are trembling. I keep walking until I see the bar I was kicked out of. More shame sweeps over me. I feel awful. I don't want to be around people, so I head home.

As I pace around my house, I think back on Sandi's presentation when she quoted Dr William Glasser, who said 'All we do is behave.' Sandi said, that essentially, from the moment we are born, we are a string of behaviours with each behaviour chosen to meet a need. Using the Phoenix Cups framework, we choose behaviours to fill a Cup. What Cup was I trying to fill when I relentlessly banged on Dan's door? It was Connection, wasn't it? I felt rejected when her store was closed so my Connection Cup was empty, and I chose a behaviour to try fill it. It was just that I chose a stupid, thoughtless behaviour, which ended up further emptying my Connection Cup. My stupid behaviour may have ended a very promising friendship.

At 11:15pm my phone rings. 'Who… who is it?' I answer, with half opened eyes.

'It's Dan. I need to say something to you.'

'Yes?' I say, wearily. I am prepared for the tirade of abuse that I suspect is coming my way, and that I most definitely deserve.

'Frank… I'm… I'm sorry. I didn't mean to be so short with you on the phone this morning. It's just that, well, without getting into too much, our last session hit a nerve for me. I don't want to go into it but I needed a day to myself, so I closed the store… Well that night, a crazed man came banging on my door. I was so frightened I had to call the police… That was a few nights ago. I've been too frightened to open the shop since… I've called you because I think you deserve an explanation. I'm sorry.'

Do I confess it was me banging on her door?

'I'm sorry to hear. When are you thinking of opening the shop again?' I ask.

'I don't know… I promise I'll call you as soon as I do though. In the meantime, I'm going to do some study on the Mastery Cup. I'll call you again soon,' she says and abruptly hangs up the phone.

For hours after, I struggle to go back to sleep. Sure, I am relieved, but guilt weighs heavily on me. I reach for Dan's husband's journal but then refrain. If I already feel terrible that she doesn't know it was me banging on her door, how much worse will this guilt be if I keep reading this private diary?

Days pass before Dan calls again.

'Would you like to come in tomorrow afternoon, and we can look over the Mastery Cup?' she asks.

'I would like that very much.'

When I get off the platform at 3:15pm the next day, the sky hangs dark and low. Like some threatening monster, it stalks me as I walk to Dan's store, spitting rain at me now and then. I find Dan behind her counter tapping away at her computer. It smells like vanilla inside the shop – has it always smelled this way?

'Hi Frank,' she says, more warmly than usual, yet with her eyes still peering down her nose onto her computer screen. 'I've got something for you.' She places her left hand onto a present wrapped in brown paper. 'It's that book by Richard Yates you were looking at when you came in for that very first time,' she says before I've even touched it.

'Wow, I didn't think you noticed. Thank you. I sure do love his writing. There's something so hauntingly beautiful in his melancholy. Speaking of writing,' I say and hold up my notebook from my people-watching at the piazza.

'Ohhh, I can't wait to see what you discovered,' Dan says, oddly vibrant again. 'How about you head back there while I quickly finish off this book order? I'm a few days behind now, so I need to send it today.'

In the back room I open my notebook up to the page that has the words Mastery Cup underlined at the top.

'So, I think an explanation is in order,' Dan says as she comes in. 'We touched on a nerve for me when we last met. Speaking of my late husband brought back some memories... He was a great man. A strong man. He didn't say much but when he did it was purposeful and always seemed so profound. This was actually his store. He would spend his days in this room writing, while I served customers out the front. We would bicker often, but boy did I love him. He just seemed to know everything. He could philosophise anything. Nothing could disrupt him. One of his favourite books is on your list. The one I showed you the very first day you came in. He had so many different copies of that damn book.'

'What was his name?' I ask.

Using her knuckles, she wipes under her eye, and whispers, 'David.'

'It sounds like he was a wonderful man.'

'I thought he was the strongest man in the world. Not physically, of course. He was only five-foot-two,' she laughs, 'but nothing could get to him, well so I thought…'

I looked over at the moleskin notebooks. David's notebooks.

'So, what have you been up to?' Dan asks with purposeful enthusiasm, to change the air.

'I spent the other afternoon people watching at a café. I watched couples interact, I watched the way some workers reacted to others, I even watched people by themselves, and what's funny is I think you can nearly see people's dominant Cups by their behaviours as easy as if they spoke them to you. It is almost as if they carry signs above their heads which show their Cups Profile.'

'Amazing.'

'While I was there, I also got started on the Mastery Cup. Here are my thoughts, if you can read my writing. What comes to my mind when I think of the Mastery Cup are words like competence, control, efficacy, power with, power within, even power over sometimes for those who don't respect the rights and needs of others. Umm, achievement, decisiveness, leadership, confidence, appearance, order sometimes. What else… fortitude perhaps. You know the other day as I got off the train, I watched a young violinist and his discipline just oozed mastery. Of course, other Cups were involved, but the way he mastered that instrument just brought this Cup to mind. While he was learning that instrument it must have been filling his Fun Cup too, until he mastered it. Now it fills his Mastery Cup. He was in a complete flow when he played. It made me see so clearly why the Fun Cup was there, to motivate him. It also made me recognise how often the Mastery and Fun Cup interact.'

'Oh wow, Frank,' Dan says.

'So, I guess, when we look at the drivers behind the Mastery Cup, they are generally those around competence, efficacy and achievement. People just choose different behaviours to gain these. I can't help but think of an old boss I had. Lovely lady, but boy was she driven to achieve. So much so, that at times she didn't realise some of the behaviours she chose had an effect on others. She was not mean by any stretch of the imagination, or inherently selfish, she just knew what she needed and went after it. Some of the other workers found her very controlling. Always kind of micro-managing. She had extremely high expectations. In a sense her need for mastery was driven to achieve self-competence. But you could not deny she was a leader; she was just that confident.'

'Would you say then that most dominant Mastery Cups are overbearing?' Dan asks.

'No, I don't think so. For instance, I think if someone had a dominant Mastery Cup and a dominant Connection Cup, their behaviour would be completely different to those who would have a dominant Mastery Cup and a small Connection Cup. It's so funny how these different Cups, or different Cups Profiles, can so affect behaviour, and therefore personality. My boss certainly had a dominant Mastery Cup, but also a large Connection Cup and a large Fun Cup, so I enjoyed her company most of the time. Actually, I can see how two people who both have a dominant Mastery Cup could conflict, and I definitely can see the confliction between those with a dominant Freedom Cup and a dominant Mastery Cup... If only everybody just understood this Cups framework, then people would not be at odds with one another. We'd understand we're all just choosing behaviours to meet our needs. If anything, we would only get upset with the behaviour, and not the person. I'm sure if we all knew our own Cups and the Cups of others, we would also choose our own behaviours more effectively without affecting the needs of others.'

'Wow, again Frank, you're certainly on a roll.'

'I can even see how if we didn't have the need for a Mastery Cup, we could easily slip into a kind of complacency. Without the drive for mastery would any of us ever accomplish anything?'

Dan puts her finger in the air to stop me, then pulls some pieces of printed paper out from underneath some books in the middle of the table. 'You know how I called you that night and was talking to you about Nietzsche and his Will to Power?' she asks. 'I think you're right, without the Mastery Cup we wouldn't accomplish much at all. Nietzsche said the Will to Power is neither good nor bad. It is just a basic, unconscious driver in all of us that has us choosing behaviours for self-competence. It's just that each person expresses it in different ways. Musicians create, scientists discover, business-minded people try to prosper. The size of the Mastery Cup is dependent on the size of the Will to Power. Some want to control others and their environment, where others might just want self-reliance. This is all the Will to Power... Nietzsche also talks a lot about self-overcoming. This is different to when people talk about finding your true self. Self-overcoming is about using the Will to Power to create your best possible self. Not in that tacky 'live your best life' kind of way, but almost in a transcendence way… I can also see how these great big Mastery Cups also change the world. I guess that goes for all the Cups. Yes, it seems society requires some of us to have each of these Cups as a dominant Cup for the greater good of the whole if you think about it. Each dominant Cup seems to serve a purpose in the self and in the community. Perhaps that's the Will to Fill at play again.'

Dan and I share a moment of silent contemplation.

'Thinking of my own life,' I say, 'sometimes I feel I am wasting away in my little flat. How life-denying my attitude seems to be sometimes. I claim to desire Mastery, however, I've been more persuaded by the easy and safe path, preferring to avoid challenges, and hide from my fears. I'm sure if I overcame them it would lead to personal growth. Not facing things leaves me in a place of anxiety, guilt and even shame. In a sense, dissatisfied. I wonder if we sometimes struggle to achieve Mastery because we are inhibited by our desire to protect the Safety Cup first?

'More often than not, however, my Safety Cup is not even at risk. I simply delude myself into thinking it would be if I were to pursue self-actualisation and Mastery. Yet if we were to fill the Mastery Cup, we'd have the self-competence we need. It's just those pesky imaginary fears, which we turn into real fears.'

'That's also extremely insightful, and brave to admit,' Dan says. Dan's praise makes me feel uneasy. I feel the need to move, so I stand and walk behind my chair – almost creating a barrier between us. My actions take me by surprise. What am I doing? I look at Dan who's just as puzzled.

'I am not brave at all. I am a coward,' I say, finally, resting my hands on the back of the chair.

'You're not a coward, Frank.'

'I am… I was afraid of my ex-wife, Jane. Not physically, but I was afraid of her scorn. She always dominated me, and I constantly walked on eggshells.'

I look over at Dan and see her mouth is open. I can't look her in the eye, so I peer down at my shoes. 'I remember the night we moved into the very first home we bought together. I'd been working away for months, and Jane was organising the move. I was supposed to join her a week later, but I pulled some strings and I was able to finish work early. Instead of calling, I decided to surprise Jane and Darlene. I can still remember opening the front door, with the bottle of champagne under my arm. I expected to find Darlene in the living room with her dolls, but she wasn't there. They must have gone back to the old house to get some more things. I placed the bottle down on the kitchen bench and went out onto the balcony. The evening air was heavy with humidity, and the trees were still, as though they were made of plastic. In this moment I couldn't help but think to myself that it was a beginning. Despite all the years of hardship, we'd made it. I'd put a roof over my family's head. Life begins now…

'It was then I heard the faint sound of laughter. I grabbed the bottle of champagne from the kitchen bench and pushed open the bedroom door. A surge of excitement came over me. Jane and Darlene must be making the bed or something. With my biggest smile I pranced into the middle of the bedroom to see a man embracing my wife on our bed. My mind raced as words of fury flew from my mouth. I couldn't even make sense of them. Jane was standing naked in front of me, screaming and punching at my face. The man had two open palms and was trying to say something calming, something nonsensical. I squeezed the bottle tight in my right hand. I wanted so badly to hit him, but I was afraid. Why was I afraid to hit an unarmed, naked man? Why couldn't I do it? Why, even in this moment of irrationality couldn't I bring myself to beat him? Why was I such a coward? I raced out of the room, and down into the carpark. I jumped into my car and screamed down the highway. As I gripped that steering wheel, I wailed hot tears into the void. I don't know where my thinking was at because I turned up at the place we were moving out of. Still crying uncontrollably, I let myself inside, found the bedroom, and squeezed myself into the darkest corner in the wardrobe. As I lay curled up in there, I gripped at the imaginary knife contorting inside my chest. I gasped for air and dry heaved until my throat burned. No matter how far I pushed myself into that corner I couldn't escape it… I didn't sleep the entire night. Instead, I ran the scene of finding them together over and over and over in my head… I lay weeping until cracks of light began to filter through, and all I could think was how dare it. How dare the sun rise as if nothing had happened... There have only been a handful of nights since then that I've been sober.'

I look at Dan and see that she has tears in her eyes. 'I don't think you're a coward, Frank. In fact, I think you are an incredibly brave man. What you've overcome with your daughter and your wife's affair, and are still standing here today, full of warmth and compassion, I think that's incredible. You're stronger than you know.'

We share a smile, but mine is feigned. Dan must sense this, or perhaps she's no longer comfortable with the emotional moment. She reaches for the notepad and a pen.

'So, to summarise,' she says, 'a dominant Mastery Cup is driven by the need to achieve self-competence. Behaviours of a person with a dominant Mastery Cup include the want for control, whether it be within, with, or over. They desire efficiency, competency, and achievement. They may be seen as confident and as a leader, though not always; whereas others with mastery as their dominant Cup may not seek the limelight but just want mastery over their own world. They could be meticulous about their own work and life. To others they may appear overbearing or even demanding, while some may look to them as inspiring.'

I nod and say, 'Do you think Mastery also has something to do with self-esteem, or do you think there should actually be a self-esteem Cup? I only ask this because I remember when Sandi Phoenix put the image of Maslow's hierarchy on the screen, there was a section in his model for self-esteem.'

Dan thinks on this for a moment, 'Maybe self-esteem is what happens when you have a full Mastery Cup and a full Connection Cup. I remember attending a conference of the brilliant Dr Louise Porter, who said something along the lines of self-competence and self-worth equating to self-esteem. Therefore, if a full Mastery Cup is a sense of self-competence, and a full Connection Cup is a sense of self-worth, then a combination of the two is self-esteem. Isn't it interesting to now see the combinations of the Cups, and how important they are to our wellbeing?'

That afternoon Dan and I order in those famous Rotis she spoke of and spend the time in idle chatter usually reserved for close friends. It had little to do with theorising the work we were undertaking but did fill the Connection Cup.

It was late when I got home, and it was probably the first night in nearly a decade that I didn't have a single drink.

JACK

12. EVEN IF YOU NEVER SAW IT

'Now, young man I am going to say something to you, and I don't want you to get upset. It's not my intent to hurt you, so I want you to hear me out.'
Beep.

    'I'm wondering what your father went through when you were taken away to the other side of the country. I'm sure losing his sons had to have affected him. He may have been a cold man, yes, but he's human none-the-less, with his own Cups Profile. I'm not saying put any blame on your mother, nor am I making any excuses for your father's actions. I'm certainly not saying his behaviour did not influence your childhood. He wronged you, yes, but sometimes we unfairly judge our parents. Are they not fallible themselves? To expect our parents to be perfect is like expecting babies not to cry, rain never to fall, or the inevitable not to happen. I know I wanted to be nothing like my old man, but I ended up hurting my daughter all the same. I never had any intention of doing so, but I did. Just as I'm sure she will make mistakes and hurt her own son. You have every right to be upset but, bear in mind, just as you felt the pain at the loss of your father, your father also must have felt the pain of your loss. Even if you never saw it.'

Beep.

Beep.

Beep.

Frank's words echo thoughts I'd hidden deep within. It's like he's holding up a mirror to a reflection I don't want to see. I have to leave the room. I don't say a word as I pass Frank's closed curtain. When I reach the hall it seems so much brighter than our room. Uncomfortably bright. I walk down the hallway, without any idea of where I am going. I soon find myself outside. I am surprised to find it's still raining. I light a cigarette, but after a drag I find that I don't want it. I take another drag and then put it out on the wet part of the metal bin lid. That moment of sizzle is distracting and satisfying, but a moment is all it is. I reach for my phone and dial a number.

'Hey, Brian,' I say when he answers.

'… Hey Jack,' he replies with a deep breath.

I realise in that moment what I've just done, calling at this time he will think that Dad has just passed.

'Dad's still with us,' I say. 'I just wanted to ask you something… How did you make peace with him? I remember it was you who stopped visiting long before I did. I remember you raging against Dad the most.'

'You're right, I did. And for a very long time I held onto that… But there comes a time, I guess, when you have to weigh it all up. I mean, was I upset he wasn't there, that he made no effort to be there for us? Sure, I was. But after a while you have to see the situation for what it is, instead of what you think it should be. When I accepted that he was my dad, he just wasn't my father, while it hurt a helluvalot, it also released me. Once I accepted that that's just how he was, it gave me peace. There's no point expecting him to be something he wasn't. There's no point holding onto pain for other people, when it's up to you to let it go. Dad can't heal your heart, only you can do that.'

I don't know how to feel. It seems like a cop-out to suddenly stop holding a grudge now. Like I've taken some easy way out. After all, being angry at him is all I know.

'You know, Dad wasn't always the monster we thought he was either,' Brian says. 'I do remember some tender moments, we've just chosen to edit those out of our memories. I remember him taking us to the beach. I remember him buying us new clothes that mum couldn't afford. He just did it all in a way we couldn't recognise as love, because he never did it with sentimentality. But he did do those things. Maybe it was because he never had a father role-model himself that he didn't really know what was expected of him.'

I can remember my father doing these things. But I've always chosen to ignore them and remind myself of the times he wasn't there. Why does this all feel so real right now? Why does it all feel so raw?

I go back inside and sit by my father's bed again. I am finding it hard to look at him. Maybe it's because if I have to acknowledge Dad as a real person, then I have to acknowledge that my father is dying.

Beep.

FRANK

13. THE FREEDOM CUP

I am still floating on a high after my last session with Dan, and I can't wait to get back and study the next Cup. Dan made it clear, however, that she wanted a few days to prepare. The next day I head into the city, down to the pier, and catch the ferry down the brown river to the suburb of Bulimba. I stroll along the main street, stopping halfway to get some choc-mint gelato. Standing out on the urban street, the gelato tastes better than any I ever remember having before. It melts quickly, and I soon find myself in a game of trying to lick around the edges before it hits my fingers. Just as I have one side sorted, the next side is threatening. I play this game until I get down to the waffle cone. That's where the treat really starts – the cold, soft ice cream mixed with the crispy texture of the sweetened cone makes me smile foolishly.

When I finish my treat I walked a few more paces and come across a barber shop. It isn't like the barbers I usually visit. Instead of a grey-haired old man, dressed in all white, the young man inside is wearing all black, has tattoos littering his arms, and his black hair and long black beard are waxed into shape. The music blares inside his shop. Lots of screaming guitars, and thumping drums. I'd never have dreamt of listening to this music, but I am loving every minute of the experience. The young man sits me down in his chair, and although I expect him to be full of bad manners, he is softly spoken and extremely polite.

I leave the barber feeling invigorated and continue to stroll until I stumble across an old theatre. I go inside and find that it still has antique charm, with high ceilings, hanging chandeliers, red velvet seats, and a scarlet curtain covering the screen, waiting for the reveal. There I watch a spooky movie of a clown terrorizing children. I am simultaneously afraid and overjoyed. That evening, as I am preparing for bed, I notice my flask is still half full.

Three days pass before Dan calls.

'Frank, I've done a lot of research on the Freedom Cup. Would you like to come in tomorrow to discuss it?'

'Of course I would… Hey Dan, what are your thoughts on looking over it somewhere else? I noticed there is a café only a couple doors down from your shop, and I think that…'

'No, I think its best we do it here. I will see you tomorrow Frank.'

I enter Dan's store late in the afternoon, bringing with me a cappuccino from the nearby café.

'I feel confident enough to tell you now that I don't actually drink tea,' I say with a smirk.

Dan looks back at me blankly, it's clear she hasn't noticed my lack of tea-drinking. She shrugs it off and says, 'I've been doing some homework for the Freedom Cup. My husband's favourite subject was actually that of freedom and liberty. I've collected some of his books which are waiting in the back room.'

'How about we work out here today? It's nice with that sun coming through your front window,' I suggest.

Dan crinkles her nose and shakes her head, and then leads the way through the purple tapestry, to the back room. As I sit down, Dan turns on the kettle and pulls down a single mug. As she makes her tea, she says, '… I can see clear as day now how big David's Freedom Cup was. Unfortunately, I can also see how much the controlling aspects of my Mastery Cup must have bothered him. It's such a pity I couldn't see it back then. I just couldn't let him be. I kept saying that he was sitting back here doing nothing while I did all the work, and I kept finding him stuff to do. He kept trying to tell me that he was working, and that his work required a great deal of contemplation. My Mastery Cup just couldn't see it. For me, work meant action.'

Dan puts her tea down in front of her seat, and before sitting down, she picks up a marker and writes Freedom Cup on the butcher's paper on the table, and circles it.

'Okay,' she says, wriggling herself into a comfortable position in her chair, 'what comes to mind for me when I think of the Freedom Cup are words like choice, creativity, curiosity, expression… hmmm what else? Independence, exploration, travel,' her eyes widen, 'experience.'

I nod and I am about to say how I can relate to all of those, when she continues.

'Oh, time alone. As in alone, but not lonely. Have you heard the word 'aloneness' before? Where loneliness is about disconnection, aloneness is about not needing anyone else. It's about being enough by yourself. Okay, what else? Authenticity, the self, or self-sufficiency, going with the flow, things like that… And I suppose if we think of someone lacking freedom, words like entrapment, and restriction. Even a dislike of responsibility comes to mind. What kind of person comes to mind when you think of the Freedom Cup?'

I lean back in my chair and put my hands behind my head. 'No one person comes to mind at the moment, but I do think of backpackers and people like that. You know, those who shrug off the norms of society and get out there and explore. They don't want to be trapped in this nine-to-five business. They want to truly experience life and spoil their senses. I know that most people feel that in some way or another, but those with a dominant Freedom Cup just seem to make it happen. Especially if they have a small Safety Cup. Then again, there are those who still wake up every day and roll into the same workplace, who must have a dominant Freedom Cup and feel utterly enslaved. They probably dream of escaping. I mean, I know nearly everyone dreams of not working and instead following their hearts, but I'm talking about those people who truly feel it. The ones who probably only turn up to work somewhere between Tuesday and Thursday, and change careers every five minutes… My cousin Mick was like that. Man, that guy couldn't keep a job down. Every few years he was doing something new. He just wanted to get out and see the world. He wanted to experience life. He hated the thought of being trapped. He thought the world had too much to offer, and his life too short to experience it all… He was once a family man too. When his wife left him and took his kids away, he reacted to it so differently to how I did when my wife left. For him, he realised that he survived the thing he feared most; losing his family. And once you have lost everything you care about, what else is there to fear? His loss ended up allowing him the freedom to fill his Freedom Cup… Wait?' I falter.

I feel as though I've stumbled onto to something, but it eludes me. As it slowly comes to me, I decide to run it through my mind before I say anything aloud. I remember once my friend Jim and I met at a bar after work. I can still see Jim clear as day, with his short back-and-sides haircut, and straight masculine jawline I was always envious of. He was swigging at his beer, while I cradled my whiskey. I even remember hearing Mick Jagger over the jukebox saying he can't get no satisfaction, which was apt for the dankness of the bar and all the dispossessed men who looked like they had it all, while being simultaneously dissatisfied with their lives. Jim leaned towards me and said, 'Your spirit's broken, that's the problem. You're off your chain, the gates open, the mailman has a limp, and it's been so long you're too frightened to chase life anymore.'

I shook my head, 'Not exactly, but I think you're onto it. It's more like an apprehension inside me, Jim. I can't explain it. It's like an emptiness, but I can't put my finger on what it is I'm lacking… To be perfectly honest, maybe I am just tired of wasting my life playing job, playing house, playing husband-in-the-suburbs. Mostly, I'm just tired of pretending that everything's okay, because no one wants to hear a complainer, right?'

Jim shrugged.

'I don't know, Jim. I mean, how could I tell my wife that I hate my job; I mean really hate it to the point where I'd rather drive off a cliff than into my parking space? Particularly when I'm the breadwinner. I have to bring home that bacon. And my friends, well, I don't want to lose face. I mean, they get up every morning just like I do, but I don't see them wanting to escape their lives. They're content to roll into the same office, or garage, or workshop for the next fifty years, and be happy to die in the same town they were born.'

Jim's eyes lift.

'I don't mean you Jim. You somehow seem to transcend all this, and I don't know how you do it. It's like your very being is an act of rebellion, and I am very envious of that… I don't know, sometimes I just hate that I was born with so much ambition, so much desire, and so many dreams. Falling short and not fulfilling any of them hurts much more than if I didn't have any in the first place.'

After a swig of whiskey, I continued, 'I mean, what am I doing with my life, Jim? Sometimes I feel I'm in so deep now that there is no surface. I hate my ordinary dreamless existence. I feel I am living someone else's dream. I'm doing what everyone else thinks I should be doing. What I thought I should be doing. I'm a sell-out. Every day I live the same old routine, and every day it gets harder and harder. You know the damnedest part of all of this? It is that I did this to myself. I didn't have the guts to live my true life. As a result, I'm lying to the world that this is me. I am lying to myself... And then there's the guilt of it all. I have my daughter, I have my health, I have a roof over my head, and so many liberties denied to others. What's wrong with me? Why can't I be happy? Why can't I just be content?'

After leaving a perfectly waited pause, Jim said, 'Congratulations, Frank. Noticing your shackles is your first step to freedom. The second is when you realise you're already holding the key.'

'I can see clear as day now that I have a dominant Freedom Cup,' I say to Dan, shaking off the memory. I move my hands from my head and cross them in front of me. 'My Freedom Cup was bone dry when I was married, because I felt helpless to fill it. My Mastery Cup must've been empty too. I was so damn concerned about my own feelings of entrapment that perhaps I neglected my wife. I remember once walking into the bedroom and catching her staring slack-jawed at the back of her veined, hardened skin, and bone-ridden hands as if they belonged to a stranger. I could almost see her weep remembering how they were once so soft and delicate. The tears wouldn't just be for her hands; they'd fall for her rounded hips, her wrinkled forehead, and for her whole wasted youth she had given over to me so easily. She must've had that same sense of something missing – an emptiness. Like she'd somehow been left behind. Unfulfilled. Lacking. Alone. She had empty Cups too. She must've despised me. I emptied her Cups.'

Dan shakes her head.

'You can't blame yourself for your wife's Cups,' Dan says, as she sifts through her pile of books on the table. She picks one up and shows me, 'This book was one of my husband's favourites on freedom. That's why I have it here today. Obviously, by the size of it, I haven't read it all. Over the last few days I just skipped to the parts that my husband used to talk about. I think it relates exactly to you and your wife, and I am sure also to millions of other people in the same situation. Clearly you both had empty Freedom Cups, we can see that. The thing is, the conflict arises because it was emptied by your own choices. Hear me out first because I'm not pushing the blame. This could be very useful to you. Jean Paul Sartre is famous for the expression "Existence precedes Essence." What he means by this is that he believes we are first born and then we find our essence, or in other words, our meaning. This is completely different to the beliefs of the past that we are born with an essence, and therefore, inherent meaning.

'You look confused. Let me give you an example: some things have an essence before they exist. A person might create a knife to cut things. Therefore, the knife had meaning before it was created. It also has the fundamental component that gives it its predetermined meaning, being a blade. Now, Sartre believes that we as humans are born and then create meaning for ourselves. He believed life itself has no inherent meaning other than what we give it. So, what has this all got to do with the Freedom Cup? Well, if life has no inherent meaning and we assign ourselves our own meaning, that means we are one-hundred percent free. We're not confined by our so-called intrinsic purpose. Normally this sounds great, "Yay freedom!", right? However, if we are one-hundred percent free, this means we have to acknowledge that we are responsible for every decision we have ever made, or chose not to make, as that is also a decision. Therefore, we are exactly where we are in life because of our choices. Now Sartre believes that this freedom is actually terrifying, that's why he says we are "Condemned to be Free". Every time you make a choice you are thereby cutting off other choices you could've made. Anxiety creeps in when we ask ourselves: what if I make the wrong choice? Anxiety is the dizziness of freedom.

'Sartre also came up with this notion of "Bad Faith". He said that bad faith is when we delude ourselves in order to spare ourselves pain in the present moment. However, in doing so this leads to long-term agony. Through bad faith we tell ourselves that the life we are currently living is the only way we can be. It gives us that entrapment feeling you were speaking about. Sometimes it's just easier to believe we are trapped by external forces because then we don't need to take ownership. We tell ourselves that we don't have any other options. We say we had no other choice… The terrifying nature of Freedom Cup filling is that if you are one-hundred percent free, then you are one-hundred percent responsible for the consequences of that Freedom Cup filling. Therein lies the nauseating paralyses of what it means to fill the Freedom Cup.'

I let out a giant breath, which I think I've been holding the entire time Dan was speaking, both frightened and entranced by what she said.

'What also brings anxiety to the Freedom Cup,' Dan continues, 'is that Freedom Cup filling is often an independent activity, with your wants, needs and desires usually different to others. Therefore, your attempts to fill it risks your Connection Cup, which in turn risks your Safety Cup. And if you do act on any of your Freedom Cup filling, you are also one-hundred percent responsible for its outcomes. We want freedom, yet we don't want to risk our love and survival. We make choices to forsake our freedom while simultaneously self-loathing for our cowardice for not filling it. If we don't have the self-esteem to self-loath, we start to blame others… You were in bad faith telling yourself you were trapped. You could have left that job, that mundane lifestyle, or even that marriage anytime you wanted. Your wife was also in bad faith thinking it was you who stole her youth. She too chose to be with you, and she chose every other decision that led her to the same point.'

Part of me wants Dan to stop. Nobody likes that kind of insight. The statements that we usually can't stomach are those that show us our own shame. Dan must sense my apprehension, as she changes the focus from me to her.

'I know too well the effects of bad faith on the Freedom Cup. Being locked in this shop for so many years, I feel completely trapped and want to break free, yet I have to acknowledge that I have trapped myself in this prison. My yearning to be free is in conflict with the fact that I am free. Therefore, I cannot blame anyone, not my husband for leaving me, not even the man who attacked me. I have trapped myself…'

Wait, her husband left? She was attacked?

'Do you want to know something?' Dan asks. 'Before I locked myself away, I was a big traveller. I loved getting my passport out and seeing the world. Sure, my Mastery Cup is my dominant Cup, but nothing gave me greater joy than to fill my Freedom Cup by travelling. Just the memory of hovering around the Malaccan World Heritage sites of Malaysia ignites a great fire in my belly. It burns even brighter picturing the faces of the vendors at the Petaling markets, or eating rotis in the streets of Penang. I still get butterflies in my stomach by closing my the eyes and recalling the cafés along Ubud's Monkey Forest Road. Even the cesspool of sleaze and filth that is Ho Chi Minh's red-light district stirs such curiosity, while my soul lifts by imagining living off the grid in Hoi An. This is where my soul burns, this is where I feel alive. Travelling is where my Freedom Cup spills over with fulfilment.'

Dan becomes aware of her wild hand gestures and replaces them in her lap. Her voice becomes as subdued as her hands, when she says, 'It's just that, ever since I became acutely aware of my need for safety, I started to forsake my Freedom Cup for my Safety Cup.'

Dan stares into the distance for a moment. I hadn't thought it at all possible that she could have a large Freedom Cup. If I had to guess her Cups Profile, I would've thought her dominant cup was Mastery, followed by Safety, then Freedom, with equally small Fun and Connection Cups. It is not that she has a large Safety Cup, it is just that it was continuously empty. Dan seems so vulnerable in this moment that although I want to ask about her husband, and about her attack, it doesn't quite seem the right time. If I've learnt anything, keeping it businesslike always seems to save Dan from those pesky emotions.

The shop bell jingles suddenly and I sense that it's a welcome distraction for Dan. She leaves the room and I strain to hear her conversation with the newcomer. When I can tell she's involved in the conversation I stand up and walk over to the small bookshelf. I take the journal out of my coat pocket and replace it to its home on the shelf and then I head back to my seat.

As I pass the door I can hear Dan's voice is distant – she must be searching for a book with the client – and for some curious reason I find myself returning to the bookshelf and pocketing the very last journal in the row. Back in my seat I reflect on what I've just done. What on earth was I thinking? As I consider returning it to the shelf, Dan re-enters the room. As a distraction, I say, 'Are we really that free though? Sure, Sartre might be right in that we are imprisoned by our own bad faith, but why then don't we feel free?'

Dan jumps at my invitation to move away from sentimentality. 'Well,' she says, 'when I was researching the Mastery Cup, whenever I searched the word Power on the internet, it always showed up this man Foucault. At the time it seemed different to the power we meant when researching Mastery. The Mastery Cup is about power within, while the power Foucault talks about is environmental, societal power. I actually didn't think it would be of use, but now I see it fits perfectly here, and I'm glad I read the article. Foucault said that previously power has been held mainly by those in command, through discipline and punishment. He said society used to have a social contract with those in power. Those in command were empowered to maintain order, through punishment of the criminals, but if they ever overstepped their mark that's when society usually revolted. Therefore, those in power came to realise that the will of the people had great influence over who was in power. This made governments extremely vulnerable. So, what evolved overtime was a three-pronged approach, which Foucault identifies as…'

Dan stops speaking and searches through the papers on the table. She finds a piece of paper with notes jotted all over it, with words and sentences facing all different angles. Some with arrows pointing to others.

'Here it is,' she says. 'Foucault said the three-pronged approach to power is through surveillance, normalisation, and examination. Today we're under constant surveillance, which has been normalised, and we're continuously examined and re-examined. This model is seen everywhere, not just by those in power, or in prisons, but in schools, workplaces, even on our streets, and online. That's what makes it so effective. And our television, movies, books, media, all this now tells us what normal is supposed to be. If the chain is long enough, a person doesn't even realise they're imprisoned. A person becomes captive by wanting to be a great student, or a great employee, or a good member of society. The worst part is we start policing ourselves. Instead of guards, we have teachers, supervisors, and social norms. We find ourselves participating whether we want to or not. We're both the supervised and the supervisors. It becomes our normal. Foucault essentially said that through surveillance, normalisation, and examination, we produce conforming, harmless and productive societies who not only follow the rules, but are satisfied with this lifestyle as a standard. People who are happy to be useful but oppressed docile subjects… I think this is what empties the Freedom Cup. People with dominant Freedom Cups recognise this is not normal, even if they can't articulate this. They just feel the oppression and sometimes they revolt. Not necessarily in anger, but by not playing the game. I think that's what has typically made those with a dominant Freedom Cups so appealing to us. They buck this idea of normalisation, and we become fascinated, or even envious of them for doing it. They're the liberated ones.'

'I guess what we call normal is what's been decided upon by the masses,' I say.

Both Dan and I take a moment for reflection.

'So why do you think we need this Freedom Cup?' Dan asks, taking me by surprise.

I ponder this for a moment, and then say, 'I think the Freedom Cup represents our need to be ourselves. That is, I think it's the drive to create our authentic self. It seems like it is that central part of us that wants to grow, and requires the experiences of life, discovery and self-reflection. Sometimes we do it through experiences and travel, sometimes through creativity, while sometimes we get it just by being alone, in contemplation. This emptying of the Freedom Cup to me sometimes feels like the restriction and denial of self-expression. I can now see where Foucault fits in, because when my Freedom Cup was empty I felt like I was playing a part in life – like I was wearing a mask. Perhaps there's an innate fear that the true me would be rejected from the world. So, I presented one to them, one that could be examined. The family man. The worker. While the real me felt cut-off. Denied. I think the drive for freedom is the drive for living authentically. Conformity is Safety Cup filling, but conformity is Freedom Cup emptying... You know I think *memento mori* could also fit in here. I think death is the only saving grace for the Freedom Cup. It's the fear of death that propels us to move forward. If we knew death was coming for us, we would worry less about conformity and seek authenticity. We would seek freedom. Autonomy. Yes, I definitely think the Freedom Cup represents our need to be ourselves.'

'I can actually see how a full Freedom Cup can spill over into the Mastery Cup as well,' Dan says. 'You're free to master yourself and your own world. I think that is authenticity.'

'Do you think evolutionary-wise, perhaps it was people with dominant Freedom Cups who were the explorers, finding new lands and provisions?' I ask.

Dan lifts her shoulders and her eyebrows, 'Maybe.' She reaches for her pen, and as she writes she says: 'The need for Freedom is the need for autonomy, for authenticity. Either freedom to do something, or even freedom from something. The means and behaviours of which are agency and choice, these just present in different ways such as travel, and what could appear like escapism or avoidance, but with the outcome being autonomy. A person with a dominant Freedom Cup might be noticeable by often changing careers, or choosing careers that are Freedom Cup filling. Such as those with a lot of independence. They probably hate to feel burdened by expectations and responsibilities.'

Dan and I sit quietly, contemplating what she summarised. The shop bell jingles again and Dan leaves the room. I find myself staring into the abyss of what we just spoke about. If I am truly free, then that means I am exactly where I am in this very moment due to every choice I have ever made or chose not to make? However, just as I am here by my own decisions, that means I can move towards wherever it is I choose myself to go. I can take ownership of this life. I can move towards whatever future I desire. Whether I get there and achieve certain things is neither here nor there, what is important is that I steer the ship. And if I live as authentically as possible, taking ownership of my choices, then the outcome doesn't really matter. My Freedom Cup will be full. I will no longer be an observer of life, I will be a participant. You are not only what you have done, but also what you choose to do next.

I shift in my chair to get comfortable and feel the journal in my pocket. I listen out for Dan and hear her in conversation, so I pull the journal out and flip it open. I flick through pages, not really reading but staring at the messy writing. As I get close to the end of the journal, however, words start jumping off the page. Words like Cancer and Terminal. It becomes instantly clear:

David was dying. I stop on a page dated 2003:

Old doc Haverford told me today that there isn't too much time left. Again, he pressed me to tell Danielle. My fear has now changed from not wanting her to worry when I first found out, to her now being mad that I left it this long to tell her. She will be furious that I didn't leave her enough time to prepare for it. Why am I such a coward?

'Look Frank…' I hear Dan's voice as she suddenly enters the room. I am so absorbed in David's words that I don't hear her coming. 'While I was talking to this customer…' She stares at the journal in my hands. Her eyes widen, and her mouth opens. She lifts her gaze to meet mine, and both her eyebrows and her lips tighten together. By her side she forms two fists.

'What are you doing?' she shrieks. 'Don't touch those! Don't you dare touch those!' She moves in and with the base of her right fist pounds me on the back of my shoulder as I turn away to cover myself. 'What are you doing looking at those?' Her voice is so sharp I can feel her hurt. 'Put it down and get the hell out of here, Frank. Get out!'

As I stand up, Dan pushes me from behind to get out of the room. I turn to apologise and see that her face is red and wet with tears. She continues to push me until I am out on the street and then slams the door shut behind me. I hear the key turning in the lock. I look behind me and can see her sobbing uncontrollably.

What have I done?

FRANK

14. ROAD TO NOWHERE

My hands shake as I bring the flask up to my mouth. How can I escape this awful feeling? It feels like I have jagged rocks in my gut. Why did I have to read those journals? Why do I make so many goddam stupid decisions? I'm a stupid, foolish old man. I put the flask to my mouth again and empty it in one quick gulp.

I pace the platform. What can I do? What can I say? Should I go back now? No, better wait till she's had some time to calm down. Goddam you Frank! No wonder your wife left you. No wonder Darlene wants nothing to do with you. You're a damn idiot.

The train arrives and I rush on in such a hurry that I fall. People gather to help me up.

'I'm fine,' I say, to a young mother trying to take hold of my arm.

When I am on my feet again she says, 'I think you should go get checked out at…'

'I don't need to go to no damn hospital. I just need to get home,' I bark at her. I notice the lady's small daughter peering out at me from behind her mum.

'I'm sorry sweetheart,' I say, but my voice still sounds manic. The girl hides her face behind her mother. I sit down and can feel everyone's eyes on me. When the train reaches my stop, I turn to the mother and thank her as sincerely as I can. She smiles back, though if I could read her mind, I am certain she still thinks I should see a doctor.

It's not until I am inside my front door that I start to feel how sore I am from the fall. I am aching everywhere. The whiskey will fix that. I take a bottle from my orange kitchen bench to the bathroom. In the cabinet behind the mirror, I find some pain killers and I down them with a mouthful of whiskey. I make my way to the couch, collapse into it and bury my face in my hands. I've really done it this time. I've really gone and messed things up.

I turn on the TV and stare at the screen without really watching it. How can I make things better? I bring the whiskey bottle up to my mouth and crunch it into my front teeth. I yelp and drop the bottle.

'Dammit.'

Most of the whiskey has run into the carpet by the time I pick the bottle up – it's in almost the same place as the spilt beer. I take what's left of the bottle to the kitchen, swap it for bourbon, and pour myself a tumbler of the brown spirit. What starts as a way to get through the night without having to face what I've done, gets me through the next three nights.

On the fourth morning as I sit on the end of my bed, my feet in my burgundy slippers, I summon the courage to call Dan. The phone rings out.

I get up and get dressed and, as I try to button my shirt, I become aware of just how much my hands are trembling. It always seems to be around the four-day mark that my body resists. I need to ease off the drink for a day. Besides, it's time to stop running away. I made a mistake and now I need to rectify it.

My determination, however, is all well and good until I get off the train at central. Much the same way a writer procrastinates with perfect preparation, I find different ways of procrastinating. I spend an hour walking around the shops looking for a present to say 'sorry'. Then over a coffee, I draft an apology letter that I'll never give her. Eventually, I catch onto my bad faith, and bite the bullet. I have to know the outcome of my pervasive actions. When Dan's shop comes into view, however, I can't go any further. I stand there for what feels like twenty minutes, just watching. 'At least her shop is open, and she hasn't shut herself away,' I tell myself. 'Maybe I'll give her a bit more time.'

That night I lay off the spirits and just keep to beer. I do the same the following night and on the sixth morning I try to call Dan again, and again it rings out. I also try to call Darlene, even though I know it's futile.

I leave it another day before I attempt to see Dan again. This time I don't have to worry about any bad faith stopping me from entering – her store is closed.

The next fortnight is a blur of drinking, attempted callings, and the occasional watching her store from across the street, chickening out every time. It's on one of the days – watching her store – that I notice something. As I lean against a pillar, a giant of a young man steps out of the store. He's youthful, maybe mid-twenties, clean-cut, and strong looking. I wonder who he is?

I finally decide to take the plunge. I lift the flask to my lips and take a long swig. I pocket it, take a deep breath, and walk across the road to her shop. The bell jingles as I step inside the store, and Dan looks up from the counter.

'I don't want to see you Frank,' she says, surprisingly calm.

'Dan. Please, just give me a moment.'

'I want you out of my shop.'

'Please, just five minutes. I want…'

'Get out!' her voice sharpens.

'Please, Dan, just five…'

'Why don't you just go find a bar somewhere, you drunk old fool?' Dan's eyes and lips elevate as cruelly as her words. I sheepishly turn around and leave quickly.

On the train ride home I feel a deep sadness. Not self-pity, not anxiety, not anger, just melancholy. The kind of low that's beyond tears, the soul level of sorrow. I sit on the train and watch as it passes my stop. I sit there for over an hour, not wanting to get up, not wanting to move at all. When the train reaches the end of the line, it takes all my energy to get off and wait for the next train home.

The last time I felt that dejected was the very first visit I had with Darlene after my wife and I separated. I remember Darlene took my hand and led me to the grey couch. She placed her small hand on top of mine as though she were the adult, and said, 'Daddy I want to tell you something and I don't want you to feel sad.'

'It's okay baby,' I said, 'you can tell me anything.'

'Okay. I think Mummy has a boyfriend. I heard someone call her "baby" on the phone.'

My poor cherub had been carrying this secret inside of her and was worried about me. I put my hand on her bony shoulder.

'I know, beautiful,' I said, and kissed her forehead. 'Are you okay?'

'I guess,' she said, and gave a chuckle to disarm the seriousness.

'Beautiful, no matter what happens with Mummy and Daddy, we'll always love you.' I kissed her forehead again and she smiled. I smiled back. Both our smiles were fake.

I remember how in the early days of those visits she would cry and cry every time I had to leave. It would break my heart so deeply. Eventually though, she stopped crying when I had to go. She began to associate me with her pain. As she got older it got harder and harder to see her. She had friends now, and in her mind I was still the man who broke up her family. I would forever have to withhold her mother's crime to spare her the pain.

I want to hear her voice so badly. I try calling again but there's no dial tone. I know for certain now that I have no way of ever contacting her. She is truly gone from my life.

That night I have a drinking session to end all sessions. To hell with Dan, and to hell with the Phoenix Cups.

FRANK

15. THE SOFT PARADE

Before I know it, July turns into October, and the trees are starting to sprout new leaves. I hadn't been to the city since the day Dan told me to get lost. Although I wasn't always in a drunken stupor, I'd reverted much to where I was at before discovering the Cups.

On the last day of the month, I am awoken in the middle of the night by a coughing fit. I cough and splutter my way to the kitchen. I grab a tumbler from the bench, throw the brown liquid into the sink, and fill the glass from the tap. My hand quivers as I put it to my mouth and scull half the glass. Even though the glass is still half full, I place it back under the tap. Suddenly I freeze. Why am I filling it up even though it is already half full? I hear Dan's words in my head: 'The Will to Fill is the empty part of the Cup, that motivates us to choose Cup filling behaviours to fill that need.'

I put the glass down on the bench and stare at it. It has been months since I've thought of the Phoenix Cups but suddenly it feels very necessary. When I was with Dan and uncovering the Cups, I felt fantastic because I was actively filling my Cups. Since it ended, I've been feeling lousy again. With Dan I was filling my Connection Cup by being with her. I was filling my

Freedom Cup by getting out of the house. I was filling my Mastery Cup by researching. I was filling my Safety Cup by feeling secure in our newfound friendship. And although we hadn't got to the Fun Cup, I found joy being in her company. Yes, I was feeling fulfilled when I was with Dan because I was Cup filling; now my Cups are empty.

I feverishly look through my cupboards for different sized glasses. When I have at least a dozen on the bench, I start to think about my Cup's Profile.

What's my dominant Cup? Freedom. I look for the biggest glass and put it in front of me.

Okay, what's my second biggest Cup? Connection. I find a cup not quite as large as the Freedom Cup and place it next in line.

What next? Safety. It's about half the size of my Freedom Cup. I search for a glass which looks about right.

Okay, now Mastery and Fun. I line up all five glasses: my Phoenix Cup's Profile.

Now, what do I need to do next? In order to fill them up, I need to determine how full or empty each of them currently is. I take each cup to the tap and fill them to the level that I feel they are at. I leave the Connection Cup empty.

Now what? I guess I need a Cup-filling plan. How can I fill each Cup with behaviours that are relevant to me? This seems more difficult… Wait, if I can determine what each Cup currently contains then that will give me an indicator of what I can do more of, or at least an idea of how to fill the rest.

I stay up for the remainder of the night coming up with a Cup-filling plan. I am writing my plan when the sun begins to rise. I remember the last sunrise I watched, the morning after I found out about my wife's affair. How I cursed that sunrise for rising as though nothing had happened, but when I watch it now I feel a sense of peace. I walk out onto my doorstep and watch the whole magnificent spectacle, as if I've never seen one before. I am struck by the thought that it doesn't matter what you go through, the sun will always rise the next day.

Over the next month I enact my Cup-filling plan. For my Freedom Cup, I make it a point to get out of my house daily. I fill my Mastery Cup by spending time at the library, researching what I can for the Fun Cup. For my Connection Cup, I rekindle my relationship with my distant brother, Henry. We haven't spoken in years, but I make the effort to call him. After burying the hatchet, we start talking nearly every third or fourth day, and we make plans to spend Christmas together in Melbourne. And finally, for my Safety Cup, I curb my drinking. Although I don't stop completely, I lower my consumption considerably, and start some light exercise, including daily walks through the park. Suddenly, I'm feeling as great as I was when I was with Dan. I know I have to try and reach out to her again.

It's a Wednesday morning, just after 10am, when I head into town. I am so determined to speak with Dan that not once do I hesitate on my trip. No bad faith, no detours, I go straight to her shop. Dan is standing behind the counter talking to the young man who I saw leave that day, only now he's behind the counter too. He notices me before Dan does, and sends me an exuberant smile, 'Can I help you, sir?'

Dan turns to face me, 'Frank?'

'Hi Dan,' I say. 'Look, I know you said you never…'

'Shh Frank, not here,' she says as she turns to the young man. 'Jackson, do you mind watching the front while I talk to Frank out the back?'

Jackson nods, and Dan waves me out the back. When we get to the room, Dan stands a distance away from me, with her arms crossed.

'Look, Dan,' I say, 'I know there's nothing I can say for what I did. I won't make any excuse, all I will tell you is that I am sorrier than I've ever been for what I did. I wronged you. I broke your trust. And even if you never find it in your heart to forgive me, I still want to thank you.'

'Thank me?' Dan asks, with a raised eyebrow.

'If you've got a moment, I'll explain why.'

Dan looks me up and down, much like she did the very first day I entered her shop, and finally nods.

'Okay, how can I best explain it?... Alright, I remember listening to the radio in my car one night, it must've been in the early seventies, when a strange man came on the air. Well he started telling the most bizarre…'

'Frank…'

'Please Dan. Let me hold the conch for just a moment. This is the best way I know how to explain what I mean.'

Dan exhales heavily through her nose.

'Well this man said if you imagine that when you go to sleep, and you slip into a dream, imagine that this one dream lasted the entire night. He said to imagine that not only did it last the entire night, but you also had complete control over everything in your dream. Even greater still, due to the time distortion of dreams, eight hours felt like an entire lifetime. The man said how at first, you would likely satisfy all your desires. I mean, you could have and be anything you want. What he said, though, is after a time, having absolutely everything go your way you would probably start to get bored. What he said is that, more than likely, we'd start to include some small challenges. After a while, even these probably wouldn't be enough, so we'd include some bigger challenges. The problem would eventually arise though, that since we knew we were in charge of the dream, the challenges wouldn't be that thrilling. What we would probably do next is choose to have some of those challenges outside of our control to keep things interesting. The problem is since we knew we were dreaming we still wouldn't be fazed, and a kind of discontent would ultimately settle in. Eventually, the man said, we wouldn't want to know we were dreaming at all. And when that moment comes, we will realise just how much that dream life is exactly like our life right now… What I am trying to say is, even if you never speak to me again, despite all this having happened, and the way things ended, having met you would still have been part of my dream life. You changed my world forever Dan, and I will be forever grateful for that.'

Dan is as still as marble, not breaking eye contact. 'You're talking about Alan Watts,' she finally says.

'No, I'm trying to tell you how I am forever grateful that even though….'

'No, I get it. That dream scenario is from Alan Watts. Look Frank that was very moving, but you really hurt me when you invaded my personal space like that.'

I drop my eyes to the floor and nod.

'Well,' she says, 'now that you've said your thing, I must also apologise. I said something pretty awful to you too… You're looking really well now, though. Better than I've ever seen you.'

I lift my stare from the ground to meet her eyes. 'Well, for a long time after I wasn't coping too well. There was a lot of drinking and self-pity. One evening, about a month ago, things changed…' I tell her all about my sunrise epiphany and my middle-of-the-night Cup-filling plan, and how I've been actively filling those Cups over the past month. When I finish, much like the first time I told Dan about the Cups when I first met her, she stays silent. The pause is agonising.

'Anyway,' I say, 'I just wanted to say how truly sorry I am, and if you ever do find it in your heart to forgive me…'

'If we are going to keep working on this together Frank, we're going to have to setup some very strong ground rules. For starters, you must never, ever invade my personal space again, nor my husband's. Secondly, you are not allowed in here if you have had anything to drink. In fact, even if you've been drinking the night before. Deal?'

My shoulders drop with a deep breath that escapes. As much as I don't want to smile yet, to show Dan that I am taking what she is saying seriously, I can't help but grin like an idiot. I don't feel like a fool for too long, as Dan's mouth slyly widens.

'I've also experienced my own personal growth while we've been apart,' she says, 'but I think I can wait to tell you that over a coffee. Would you like to meet for coffee on Sunday, at the café a few doors down? My nephew, Jackson, will join us. While he plays on Facebook, you and I can discuss the Fun Cup.'

FRANK

16. THE FUN CUP

It's just after 1pm when I meet Dan and her nephew at the café. The walls are lined with coarse and irregular red bricks, the roof has large exposed yellow light bulbs, and copper pipes run along the ceiling. What isn't made of wrought iron and copper, is made from timber. The waitress wears denim overalls and a striped yellow T-shirt. She has black hair with a straight fringe which offsets her wonderful freckles and dimples when she smiles. What I thought were stickers on her arms are actually tattoos, much like the ones I used to only see on the toughest sailors, who I was worried would seduce my girlfriends.

Dan and Jackson are hidden away in the back corner of the café. When I reach their table, Jackson stands up to shake my hand, like a true gentleman.

'That's a strong grip, son. I'm glad you were taught how to shake a man's hand,' I say.

'Frank, this is my nephew Jackson. Jackson, this is Frank.'

'Pleased to meet you Frank,' Jackson says.

'Likewise. And how old are you, young man?' I ask, as I sit down.

'Twenty-two. No wait, twenty-one.'

'And what's your story?'

'Well my mum thinks I should study. She said maybe business management or something. Mum thought it might be a good idea to come work with Aunty Dan in her shop, you know, to get some real experience. When Aunty Dan said it was okay, I moved up here from Sydney. That was about three months ago now, wasn't it?' he asks, looking at Dan.

'About that,' Dan says, studying the menu.

There's a naivety about Jackson that's charming. He's not a dullard, but endearing and young for his age. Jackson would be guided by Dan, while simultaneously keeping her safe – whether he knew that was his role or not.

'Anyway, I've got to go call my girlfriend. Are you fine if I go outside?' Jackson says to Dan, who nods. He then gets up and leaves the café.

'So, I guess we have a lot to catch up on,' Dan says.

'Yes, well you said the other day about some transformations you've had. I can't wait to hear about those,' I prompt, gesturing with my hands to our surroundings.

Dan nods, and smiles in a restrained way. It's as though she thinks a full smile would reveal a crack in her armour.

'Well after our… altercation,' Dan says, 'I closed the shop for a few days. I was done with you, I was done with the Phoenix Cups, and I was nearly done with this city. I called my sister in Sydney, I was thinking of selling the shop and moving in with her. After a few hours on the phone she reminded me of a few things. One: I've had this store for nearly twenty-six years. I can't give it up. Two: after being on the phone with her for just an hour there would be no way in hell I'd be able to live with her. And three: I needed to move forward not backwards. Anyway, the conversation meandered as they do between sisters, and she told me how she couldn't get her son…' Dan looked out the window at Jackson, who had his face buried in his phone, 'to do anything with his life. She thought it might be a good idea if Jackson flew the coop for a little while. Maybe see what it's like out in the real world. She thought it might give him a little motivation. At first, I resisted, but my sister pleaded and used my words against me. She knew I needed change, and promised it would just be for a while. A few days later this mountain of a boy clumsily arrived on my doorstep. For the first few weeks he struggled with me not leaving the store…' the barista interrupts, placing our coffees on the table. 'One Sunday morning, when he was trying to get me to come out for breakfast, he said, "It's the middle of the day. You're safe. Plus, you're with me. I've been boxing since I was nine, I'll protect you." I still said no. He then said something extremely insightful – though I am not sure he was really aware of how profound it was. He said, "Are you scared of seeing people, or are you scared people will see you?" And that's when I realised, I've been hiding in my store not only because of fear for my safety, but also because I no longer wanted the world to see me… It's about time I told you some things Frank.'

Dan cradles her coffee mug with two hands and lifts it to her lips. She looks around us to make sure we have privacy, 'I remember saying to you once during one of our sessions just how strong I thought you were, for what you had shared with me about your divorce. Well, if only my husband could've been that strong. Really, that's what kills me the most. To me he seemed like the most competent man in the world. I adored him. I thought he could handle anything, and that gave me strength…' Dan drops her gaze to her mug.

'One month he suddenly started brooding a lot. Of course, he was an armchair philosopher, so I had some experience with this, but this was different. He grew incredibly distant. I would catch him in that back room where we've been studying, and instead of scribbling away in his notebooks, he would just stare off in thought. Whenever I'd approach him about his mood, he'd fly into a rage… One night, when I was locking up the shop, he told me he would meet me at home. He did this sometimes, particularly when he was on a roll with his work. After dinner he still wasn't home. After my shower he still wasn't home. After an hour reading in bed, he still wasn't home. I must've fallen asleep, because when I woke in the morning he wasn't in bed next to me.

'I was both furious and panicked. I hurried to the shop and when I went to open the front door, I could see that it had been barricaded from the inside by one of my large bookshelves. A stranger off the street who could see my distress helped me push the door hard enough to move the bookcase. I raced into the room and found him; he was leaning back in his chair and his mouth was open. On the table was an empty packet of pills... There was no note.' Dan runs a knuckle under her right eye, brushing away a tear. 'This was the man I loved and admired, the man who could handle anything. And if he couldn't handle this life, what chance do I have?

'That year I lived life on a pendulum. I was either numb and indifferent, barely existing, or I was in a rage, cursing everything and everyone. David included… Then one night, I was locking up the store, and on the way to my car I was approached by someone wearing a hooded jacket. I remember his menacing, frightening voice saying "Give me your bag now and I won't hurt you. But if you make a sound I won't have any other choice." His mugging emptied my Mastery Cup by taking away all my power and control, and threatened my Safety Cup… Unfortunately, this wasn't the first time someone has threatened my safety. My father was a mean drunk. The problem is he wasn't smart enough to know he was a monster. In his mind it was always us that made him act out. He would say that we shouldn't have provoked him even though he gaslighted and pushed us until we reacted. Then he would take his fury out on my mother, and my sister and me. We were his slaves. We cooked his meals, washed his clothes, and lived in a constant state of stress and anxiety. He used to say that we needed to respect him. What he didn't realise is that yes, we feared him, but there is a big difference between fear and respect. We certainly didn't respect him. Any regret that would eventually surface from him was always short lived, as were his promises of change… After I escaped, I never wanted to see any of my family again. Not that it was my sister or mother's fault, I just didn't want to be reminded of any of it… Anyway, after the attack from the mugger, I got my cousin, who is a carpenter, to build a bedroom and a bathroom up the back of the store for me. Until a month ago, I hadn't left that building in over four years.'

I want to reach out and hold her and somehow take some of her pain away. She must sense this because she smiles and says, 'Small Connection Cup remember, keep that hug to yourself… Now those journals. To me it feels like those are the last place David is still alive. I've never read them. I'm terrified that if I read them that I will hear his voice in my mind, and I will miss him all the more. Or, more frightening than that, what if I don't hear his voice? What if I've forgotten what it sounds like? I guess when I saw you reading his journals, it frightened me. When they were sitting there unread, it felt like a part of him was still there: alive. Once they've been read though they become only a memory of him. Perhaps, that's another reason why I can't read them.'

At that point a young man comes to our table. He has a beard much like the barber who cut my hair, as well as hair slicked to the side. He's wearing a red and black checked flannelette shirt, looking like he'd be better suited to a timber yard than a café. He kneels down, so that he's at our level, and asks if we've had enough time to study the menu.

Dan orders a toasted croissant and I ask for the same.

'So, you have to tell me, when did you leave your store?' I ask.

'Well, for a while I couldn't stop thinking about what Jackson had said about not wanting to be seen. Not only that, the Cups came to mind. I was thinking over the Freedom Cup and the Safety Cup, and I realised just how important they were, how I had been neglecting them all these years and how I wasn't fulfilled – I was just experiencing a lack of suffering, as Schopenhauer so eloquently put it. I knew I had to fill my Cups, and I knew the only way to do that was to do what I have been fearing the most. Now I don't know if it was fortuitousness or not, but a customer came in and ordered Dr Susan Jeffers book, *Feel the Fear and Do it Anyway*. Well, when it came in, I read it cover to cover overnight. It was then that I decided I had to finally leave the store. I made a plan with Jackson. The first day all we did was take a step out the front door. Even then, I felt dizzy and overwhelmed. It was like the street was brighter, louder, more ferocious than I ever remembered it. The next day was the same. The day after that, the emotions I felt were somewhat reduced. The following day, although we only stayed the same distance, we waited out there for a while longer. Each day we took a few more steps. After a fortnight, we'd made it down to this café to order takeaway coffees. I was scared that day. People's movements seemed so erratic. Everyone was so hurried. The music was loud, causing everyone to have to raise their voices. We did this coffee run a few times. One afternoon we even quickly looked at the dress shop between my store and here. After a few more weeks, I finally gathered the courage to eat here. This is the third Sunday in a row now that we've had breakfast here. As yet, I haven't gotten any further, but it's a giant step for me.'

I so desperately want to reach forward and take hold of her hands. Instead I give her my warmest smile.

'I became fascinated at just how much better I was feeling by making it just this far. I worked out what was making me feel so good was that my Freedom Cup was getting filled. So, for the past three weeks I've been feverishly studying the Phoenix Cups again. And then low and behold, you show up at my door, Frank.' For the first time in our relationship, Dan smiles openly at me.

'Well, how about we look at those Cups now?' I suggest.

Our croissants arrive. Dan tears a small piece off her croissant and places it her mouth.

'To be honest,' she says, 'the studying I've been doing has been on the Cups we've already discussed, I haven't yet looked at the Fun Cup. What I did discover, however, is that Dr William Glasser's Choice Theory didn't have outcomes for the basic human life needs. What I think is that each Cup in the Phoenix Cups framework actually has a different outcome. Some we touched on by accident by calling them drivers. I was actually going over the notes for the Safety Cup, when I saw that I wrote that the outcome of a full Safety Cup is Security. It got me thinking, what then would the outcome be for the Freedom Cup? Then it hit me, of course, Autonomy. I did the same for the Mastery Cup, which I think is Self-Competence, and the Connection Cup is Self-Worth. What makes me so sure about this is when we mentioned Dr Louise Porter saying self-esteem is self-competence and self-worth together. Or in other words, having a full Mastery Cup and a Full Connection Cup. Since I haven't yet looked over the Fun Cup, I haven't determined it's possible outcome. When I think of Fun though, I really can't help but wonder why it is important? And is it really an innate need?'

'Well,' I say, 'I mentioned to you how I've been doing research at the library. Through my studies I definitely believe Fun is a basic human life need. What astonished me was stories of people in conflict, even war zones, still choosing to have fun at times even when it can put their lives at risk. Or even skydiving and other extreme sports, for example. People are choosing fun that is directly putting the Will to Life at risk. So, it definitely exists as an innate need, but why is it there? I decided to look at the purpose behind the need. To do that I needed to ask what is fun? I discovered that fun is essentially just brain chemistry that allows us to experience pleasure, making it fundamentally biological. Why? Well it has to do with the learning. Fun imprints memory. I decided to research Glasser. It turns out he said "fun is the genetic reward for learning", it ensures we seek out this pleasure – this continuous learning. Well, it got me thinking about the man I saw who'd mastered the violin. Clearly fun was required, otherwise he would not have pursued the instrument to reach mastery. Now I can clearly see children's need to play a lot. When they play they learn about their world. It took me a bit longer to determine why we need fun and learning as adults though.'

Dan's leaning forward on her elbows, clearly impressed. I feel myself sit straighter in my chair.

'Now we may not think we're filling our Fun Cup when we learn,' I continue, 'but have you ever been forced to study something you didn't want to study, versus studying something you were interested in? Time flies when you study your interests; you retain more, and it's painless. The absence of pain is not pleasure, but it is still Fun Cup filling, that's probably why sometimes it feels so elusive. You could be Fun Cup filling without even realising it.'

'Very impressive, you've got me thinking. Clearly, I look like someone who has a tiny Fun Cup. I don't smile much, and sometimes, dare I say, I even find laughter to be the most awful sound in the world. Yet, in saying that, I find fun in so many different ways that you may not initially recognise. Food, for instance. Food brings me great pleasure. If I were to eat for survival, I wouldn't care what I put in my mouth. Like what you were saying about yourself with your daughter. When I eat, I fill my Fun Cup and my Freedom Cup. I love food from different parts of the world. Food excites me. Food liberates me. And before I was a shut-away, I used to love sharing my dining room table with friends – so food also connected me. Needless to say, food fills my Cups. So, I guess we cannot always see the Fun Cup being filled.'

Dan looks up suddenly towards the door of the café. I turn and see someone wearing a jacket with the hood up over his head. When I see he's just a tall child, I turn back around. Though she says nothing, I can sense the relief in Dan.

'Well, what else I discovered,' I continue, trying to distract her, 'is that we could also say that play stimulates our minds, increasing brain function, which surely could only be a good thing for adaptability, and problem solving. Play can also improve our social lives, with increased connection ensuring our survival. One study even said that fun and play can also increase empathy for one another, trust, and compassion. I would also go so far as to say play alleviates stress to allow us to be more productive. Yes, I believe play is extremely biologically-driven. I suppose even as far as mating and the Will to Life. We find courtship fun. Therefore, I think the need for the Fun Cup makes perfect sense, even for adults.'

'Frank, I'm not used to you doing all the work, but I am loving this. You've really got a grip on this one.'

I can't contain my smile, 'You could even say I was motivated by fun to research this Cup. It was while researching alone that nostalgia really crept in. I was sitting in the library wishing it was your back room, and I discussing all this with you. I thought on all the different angles we would be tackling this Cup from, when I realised I hadn't looked at it philosophically, as you would have. I certainly didn't know where to start, so I asked the librarian. He was stumped too, so I fumbled my way through the philosophy section for days. Eventually, I came across what I needed. Well, it turns out many of the early philosophers believed that all we really desire is happiness as an end in itself. And that all other things we desire are just means of producing that happiness or clearing the way towards that happiness. Often we spend our lives unconsciously chasing happiness, but we just get confused about what we think will make us happy. This is because we confuse pleasure with happiness, contentment, or joy. Pleasure is something entirely different and often leaves us in more pain. This is where it gets exciting, Dan. I discovered a Hellenistic philosopher called Epicures, who spent his time wondering *what makes people happy?* Epicures noticed that there are both necessary and unnecessary desires. Necessary desires are those that free us from bodily pain, even as simple as quenching a thirst with water. How pleasurable and necessary can a drink of water be when you are thirsty? Unnecessary desires are things like excess riches, fame and luxury, which can all produce unhappiness. For example, to make more money than you require usually means you have to work harder. But once you make beyond what you need, excess money often does not increase happiness. All the sacrifice required to get it, the loss of time with loved ones gone, and for what? To buy more stuff? We can even see today that advertising makes us feel we're missing something. That we always need something more. That happiness, and joy, and contentment exists on the other side of whatever it is they're selling. Epicures believed having more of anything than what is needed is no more useful than an overflowing container – or Cup, in our case. If you place your happiness in unnecessary pleasures you'll be anxious to obtain them, scared to lose them, and continuously pushing towards more, causing great anxiety and disappointment... I discovered a book by William Irvine who writes about the concept of Hedonic Adaptation. Essentially, it is about our insatiable desire to have more. But once we have whatever it is we desired, after a time we grow bored of it and take it for granted, and then strive for more again.

'How often have we bought a piece of clothing, loved it intensely, and then after a few years find it tucked away in the back of the closet? This can include not only objects, but even lifestyle and relationships. Who hasn't chased a certain career, only to have grown dissatisfied with the job after a time? Even the lover we once courted, whose flaws we adored at the beginning, now start to irritate us. So, I guess Hedonic Adaptation is the boredom we feel towards whatever it is we have obtained which we once desired, and now crave more. Irvine says somewhere that we forget that we're already living the dream life; our dream life. A life we once desired. We've just adapted to it. We strive to gain more, thinking that this stuff will fill our Fun Cup. But just as a little wine might make us feel good, too much wine causes dizziness and a hangover. Essentially, Epicures believed you are better off eliminating an unnecessary desire, than causing too much pain working to satisfy it…

'I agree to an extent, but I also think mindfulness comes into play. I believe you can enjoy certain pleasures if you are consciously aware of them. Aware enough to ensure that they cause you no harm, nor any harm to those around you. Sometimes though, this takes a certain level of foresight. So, what comes to mind when you think of someone with a dominant Fun Cup, Dan?'

'Hmm, when I think of someone with a dominant Fun Cup, I think of those who always seem to smile and laugh. You know, they often appear less stressed too. Whether they are or not, I'm not so sure, but they certainly look like it. They just seem full of joy. Wait, that's it. The outcome of a Fun Cup is Joy. They experience joy and can bring that joy to those around them… When I think of filling the Fun Cup, I think of filling it wisely with friends, laughter, learning, play, contemplation, and simple pleasures. I think the Fun Cup is a fairly intuitive Cup to fill actually. What I think we need to do is learn how to fill it effectively without affecting others or causing ourselves any corresponding pain which Epicures warned us about. I guess that can go for all of our Cups.' Dan stops speaking and looks me dead in the eye. Instead of her usual intensity though, she pulls a sideways smile.

'What?' I ask.

Dan pulls out an unsealed envelope and hands it to me. 'Here, I got you a present.'

'What is it?'

'Open it,' she says.

I open the envelope to find a ticket inside.

'Guess what?' Dan asks. 'The Phoenix Cups team are coming back to town, and this time instead of speaking on the Cups for children's behaviour, Sandi Phoenix is telling her own story.'

'That's fantastic! Please tell me you'll come with me?'

Dan shows me both of her palms, the universal signal for 'stop'. But instead of anger, or fear, she laughs, 'No, no, no, no, no,' she says.

'Dan, you have to come with me. This has been our thing. I'll be by your side the entire time… Imagine how Cup filling it would be?' I press.

'Not going to happen, Frank,' she says. 'Now, listen, I want another week to myself before you come back. I want a week so that I've had enough time to research everything on that piece of paper that man wrote for you, and also come up with what I think he meant by saying: "Only you can fill your Cups. Only you can create your own meanings."'

FRANK

17. CUPS AND RESPONSIBILITY

On my week away from Dan, I continue filling my Cups. I go back to the barber in Bulimba and get my haircut. I also join the local gym, which has a lap pool, so I can get back into swimming. I experiment with cooking, trying out different cuisines and flavours. I even spend time in the botanical gardens, exploring as many senses as I can; I study the colours of the flowers and the grass, feel their textures with my fingertips, and watch the busying of the bees and the interaction between other insects. I see worlds within worlds.

I spot a lady beetle underneath a leaf. It strikes me that I almost missed it and I consider the notion that things exist outside of my own experience, and that all I can actually experience is representations of these things; that is, I can only perceive the world through my limited senses. There's even a world within me: my organs and even microorganisms, and within my mind and thoughts. That means others can only perceive and not experience me too. I think about that fellow, Schrodinger, and how in his thought experiment his cat is simultaneously alive and dead. Does this mean I simultaneously exist and not exist?

I can feel a sense of loneliness and melancholy begin to rise, but another thought comes to me, and I suddenly feel very unique. There are certainly things about me that are real. I was born, I have two arms and two legs. These are the facts about me. There are also other things about me that are not yet real, like what I choose to do next. Having done them, however, these will then turn into facts about me... Wait, does that mean my Cup filling is less dependant on what I currently am, and more on what I choose to do next? Does that mean in a sense my Cup filling is unique and limitless? How liberating.

When I return to Dan's after a week, she pulls me inside quickly and locks the door behind me.

'Oh my god, Frank, I can't wait to show you this.' She pushes me forward as a child might to a parent when motivating them to come see something.

'Dan, it's 9:30am, you need to stay open for your customers. Where's Jackson?' I ask.

'Shhh, don't worry about any of that. I did so much research on everything left on that note and contemplated what was said to you: "Only you can fill your Cups. Only you can create your own meanings." What I think he meant was that your Cups are your responsibility. Now trust me, it's deeper than it sounds.' Dan pushes me into the back room, only now it's different. The heavy curtains that had always been closed were open, and dust rode the great beam of light that spilled in and bathed the table. Darkened corners of the room were illuminated, probably for the first time in years, and all the junk mail had been removed from the corner. The room was alive again, while outside, the sounds of the bustling streets could be heard.

'This is amazing,' I say.

Her face lights up, and her eyes take the shape of almonds.

'Wait until you see what I've discovered,' Dan motions for me to take a seat but she remains standing. 'What the man was talking about is essentially fulfilment. I know we have mentioned it before, but we didn't see the context in which the Phoenix team meant it. They're not talking about some grand mystical fulfilment that only seems to exist in the future. They're also not talking about one that, once found, means life is complete. They're talking about those momentary fulfilments that can be achieved in this lifetime and this present moment. The only way this is possible is for us to take ownership of our Cups, because how full or empty they are will ultimately come down to us. Therefore, fulfilment is up to us. Not fulfilment as in your world is perfect now, but fulfilment in the sense that our basic human life needs are being met, or that at least we know how to get them met. A more real, and humanistic fulfilment.'

Dan makes circular motions with her index fingers, as though trying to find the right words. 'It's basically saying "right now I have all the outcomes of the Cups met." I have joy, self-competence, autonomy, security, and self-worth, and I need nothing more. Or at the very least, I know what I can do to achieve those outcomes. It's okay if this doesn't make complete sense right now, just hear me out.'

'I think you've lost your mind,' I laugh.

'So, I researched some of the names on the page and one of them was a Roman slave named Epictetus, who lived around two-thousand years ago. The interesting thing about this slave was that he was born into slavery. One story even notes that his master may have broken his leg as a boy, leaving him lame for the rest of his life. Now we could easily imagine how difficult life would've been for a slave two-thousand years ago. This slave was fortunate enough, however, to be around numerous philosophers, and when he finally gained freedom much later in life, he started his own school. The incredible part is, despite living this extremely difficult life full of hardship, what he came to realise was something phenomenal. He realised that what usually upsets people are not things themselves, but their *judgements* about things.

'What he's essentially saying is that things are just things, and events are just events. They don't upset us, we upset ourselves by the way we think about them. That is, our judgements about them. Let me think of an example... Okay, let's use your train ride home every day. Ever notice how a late train seems to bother some people more than others? If you're in a hurry to get home, you'd be more upset by a late train than somebody who doesn't even want to go home. Therefore, it's not the late trains that upset us, we upset ourselves through our judgements of them. If it truly was late trains that upset people, they would upset everyone equally. You might be upset, but the teenager who doesn't even want to go home might be glad it's running late.'

'Yeah, I see what you mean,' I say, 'and this is all well and good for the trivial stuff, but you can't tell me this is possible when things really go wrong. What about the big stuff?'

'Well, I won't pretend to assume this applies to all trauma, nor am I belittling traumatic experience. Terrible, horrible things happen in this world. Let's look at a case, though, of someone taking ownership of their thoughts and judgements in extreme traumatic conditions. One of the other names on the page was the holocaust survivor, Viktor Frankl. In his book, he talks about losing his wife and family in the most horrible of circumstances in World War II. He also talks about the years he spent in the Auschwitz concentration camp undergoing the most horrendous treatments. In his book, *Man's Search for Meaning,* he describes horrors I pray no one will ever have to live through again. He writes about his time there and about finding meaning, even in suffering. He said that when he found meaning in his suffering, he didn't even bother to alleviate that suffering anymore. Now, even after experiencing these traumatic events, he was able to say, "Everything can be taken from a man but one thing: the last of the human freedoms; to choose one's attitude in any given set of circumstances." What he's saying is that even in the worst of conditions – in conditions I hope you and I will never have to be tested to even think that way – is that whatever happens to you does not need to affect you unless you choose to let it. I think the key word in there is choice. He chose to think a certain way… Again, I am not depreciating trauma at all, but wow, right? Viktor Frankl is a testament that this kind of thinking is possible.'

'Okay, I am following,' I say. 'But what's this to do with the Phoenix Cups?'

Dan finally takes her seat. 'Here's how I think it relates: The way we think about things affects the way we feel about things. And the way we feel about things affects the way we behave. This isn't particularly new knowledge. But if we look at that in Cup language, it's far more inclusive than an algorithm of "thoughts create feelings, feelings create behaviours", because with the Cups we now have five motivators. So, we could say that the way we think about things, affects how full or empty our specific Cups are, which then affects the way we behave, because as we know every behaviour is to meet a need – or fill a Cup. Therefore, we need to be careful about our thinking to ensure it is Cup filling and not Cup emptying…'

I think about this for a moment. Running her words over in my mind.

'During my research,' Dan continues, 'I found a list on the internet of what are called Unhelpful Thinking Styles. These are different thoughts that seem to upset us in different ways.' Dan shuffles through the pages and books on the table. 'Ah, here's the list… For example, when we apply a Mental Filter, instead of seeing the whole picture, we only focus on negative details. Or, in Jumping to Conclusions, we assume we know what others are thinking or what some unknown outcome will be. There are a ton of them. Over-Generalising, Personalisation, Catastrophising, Labelling, Emotional Reasoning, Should's and Must's, and Disqualifying the Positive. These are all thoughts that make us feel a certain way or exacerbate situations, and ultimately empty our Cups. For example, thinking "no one loves me" - which would be over-generalising, catastrophising, using emotional reasoning, and labelling - would empty my Connection Cup. By acknowledging that I have the love of a few close friends, or that I am part of a community or workplace, would be Connection Cup filling. This thinking can affect all our Cups, including the psychological aspect of the Safety Cup. If we are catastrophising, thinking that, say, if tomorrow we're late for a mortgage payment we would automatically become homeless, this would clearly be Safety Cup emptying. But if instead of catastrophising, we thought realistically, we would see that it's unlikely that event would happen. As a result, our Safety Cup would not be as affected. So, it's not really about removing unhelpful thoughts, it's about learning not to empower them. Our Cups are therefore our responsibility, as they are a result of our own thinking and our actions.'

'Hmm,' I say. 'That seems a bit unfair sometimes.'

'Okay, well this brings me to the next point. Epictetus, the same slave philosopher, also said that "Happiness and freedom begin with a clear understanding of one principle. Some things are within your control and some things are not." Now what he means by that is if we want peace, we should only concern ourselves with that which we can actually control. So, what can we control, Frank?'

'Umm, ourselves. How our friends see us… How much we…'

'There are only two things we can control, Frank. Our thoughts and our actions. We can have certain levels of influence over external things but, really, we cannot control anything other than ourselves. We cannot control other people. We cannot control what they think, or do, or say. We cannot control them any more than we can control the falling of the rain, or an earthquake. We certainly cannot control if our train is late, but we can control how we respond to our train being late, by the way we think about it. Getting annoyed over such things will not change the outcome, only empty our Cups.

If we ever try to wager our happiness on things outside of our control, there's always a chance we will come off second best. It is not to say we don't care about these things, and other people, we still do our best. It's about acknowledging that we can only control ourselves in any given circumstance.'

Dan trails off and looks at the moleskin journals on the shelf. After a moment, still staring at the journals, she says, 'I accept now that I couldn't control the motives of the man who attacked me; all I can do now is control how I respond to what he did, what I do next with my thoughts and my actions. So, I am not talking about just forgetting what happened and moving on, no, I am talking about moving forward…' She turns her attention back to me. '… I guess what I am saying is that we don't have a thousand competing concerns. In every single situation, we only ever have two concerns, our own thoughts and our actions. It's not up to us what others do. It's only up to us how we respond to it. So, Frank, letting go of all these things you cannot control offers you peace.'

Leaning my elbows on the table, I bring my fingertips up to cover my mouth. It just seems so unfair. Why does it seem unfair though? Is it because by acknowledging this I then have to take some responsibility for my feelings?

'Sometimes, though, I worry that if I stop worrying then something bad will happen,' I say.

'I understand. I, too, often think that if I stop worrying about certain things, something worse will happen. The thing is, it's already outside of my control, so worrying about it will not change the outcome. It will only empty my Cups. And it will be me who emptied my Cups by the way I thought about it.'

'Hmm, this all sounds very passive,' I say.

'Well, we often mistake worry for action. Often, we sit around worrying but don't actually do anything. So no, it isn't about giving up and being passive, it's about acceptance. It's about letting go of what's outside of your control and transferring all that time and energy you wasted on worrying into doing your best in the moment. It's about accepting outcomes, knowing that you did your best. You see, Frank, you cannot always control the situation, but you can control how you respond to that situation through your actions and the way you think about it.'

'Hell,' I say 'what about my wife? My wife smashed my Cups. My daughter not returning my calls, or letting me see my grandson, surely this is Connection Cup emptying.'

'Frank, what your wife did was outside your control. You cannot blame yourself, as much as she cannot blame you. We're all responsible for our own actions. Your daughter ignoring you is also outside of your control. What's in your control is how you respond to all that now. Don't let yesterday's pain empty your Cups today, Frank. All you can do is focus on what you can control right now. Now is where life exists. Not yesterday, not tomorrow. Right now.'

I need a moment to think on this.

'Okay, I get that our thoughts empty our Cups, and our thoughts to an extent are under our control, but we are still human beings, Dan. Surely stuff will still get to us. And what about social justice things?'

'Of course, things will still get to us. We just need to ensure they don't overrun us. We need to keep them in check. We will still have our moments, but there's no point turning them into more than they need to be. There's no point allowing something to empty more of our Cups than it should. You see, sometimes when we complain about something, we feed it. When we catastrophise and rant, we snowball it from something relatively minor, which should have only taken a splash out of our Cups, into a Cup-emptying event. Again, I don't expect us to be this calm and in control just yet. All this requires mastery, though I'm sure for the sake of our Cups it would be a mastery worth pursuing. In terms of social justice, you can still fight just as hard for any worthy cause without letting it affect your Cups. If anything, that would make you more powerful. Have you ever noticed the angrier you get the more your brain function shuts down? Your anger literally makes you dumber. However, having full Cups makes you a force to reckon with. So, do all that you can absolutely do, and push forth as best you can with advocacy, then you can rest at the end of the day knowing you have done all that you could.'

I think about what Dan has said. It's as though a part of me doesn't want to believe it.

'This all makes sense, as I said, but a man at Central Station once yelled abuse at me just before I got on my train. What about that situation? I know I can't control him, but he still upset me.'

'Okay, now I am not talking about acts of violence or abusive people, I'm talking about non-dangerous situations. Let me guess, after that man said that stuff to you, instead of brushing it off, you probably had a little imaginary argument with him in your mind. You probably thought up the best comeback, but it was too late. This probably angered you even more. Well as you can see, you are emptying your Cups more by the way you continue to catastrophise this event. That is, the way you're thinking about this event. For instance, if you were having a crappy day, his words might have upset you more than if you were having a great day. Therefore, it is not the man's words but your judgements of them. If that man were a child and said the same words, it might not bother you as much. You can't control other people, only how you respond to them. Trust me when I say this Frank, I'm not saying I am up to this level, but it's definitely something I want to work towards, because my Cups are my responsibility. I want to take ownership of my life. How I feel about my life will be dependant one-hundred percent on me. I refuse to tell my Cup-emptying story any longer.'

'What do you mean by story?' I ask.

'Our story is the little narrative we tell ourselves inside our minds of who we are now, based on the events of our past. For instance, if a parent was cold to us growing up, or if an early lover chose someone else over us, we might tell ourselves the story that we are now unlovable in the present moment. This story, however, is an over-generalisation of our past which would be Connection Cup emptying in the present. We all carry around all sorts of stories which kind of play on autopilot. What happens, though, is we put on a lens when we tell ourselves our stories, and just like the unhelpful thinking styles, we rarely analyse our stories for any truth. People tend to take their own perceptions of the reality of the world… Believe it or not but my older sister, Jackson's mum, is even more sullen than I am. Now, although we shared the same childhood, had the same advantages and disadvantages, our stories are different because of the lenses we choose to view them by. For instance, her story is that she is hard done-by. She works harder than everyone else, and she is unappreciated. She feels that life treats her unfairly, as though the universe were somehow able to conspire against her and bend the laws of nature to push her down. Now I'm being a tad harsh to make the point, God knows I'm not an optimist either, but it shows how our stories can affect who we are in the present moment. I agree that life can be very tough sometimes, but it's tough for everyone, despite what we may see. The universe didn't conspire against my sister; the universe is indifferent to my sister, as much as it is to me or anyone. My husband always quoted the philosopher, David Hume, who once said that the universe cares as much about you as it does for an oyster… Whatever has happened to me, has just happened to me. And when an event happens in our life, we don't have to make it our story.'

I think back on the last twenty years of my life. Have I just been telling myself a Cup-emptying story this entire time?

'If we want to find some level of contentment, we need to ask ourselves if our stories are serving us.' Dan interrupts my thoughts, almost as though she's reading my mind. 'Your wife's affair, which tore apart your marriage, and resulted in the loss of your family, definitely matters. But how you choose to make it a part of your story now is completely up to you. You can't control what she did, but you can control how you respond to what she did by controlling that part of you which are your thoughts and your actions. Therefore, you can make the event a Cup-emptying story, or you can choose to make it an empowering story of overcoming, and it can be Cup filling. Remember, you write the script to your life. Just because you've been thinking a certain way your whole life doesn't mean it's true. You're allowed to challenge your thoughts which means you're allowed to change your story anytime you like. So constantly ask yourself, is my story Cup filling or Cup emptying?'

I take a deep breath. Dan and I share a moment of silence.

'You know what, Frank? This may very well be our one and only life. And life exists in this moment. The world has been around for billions of years and will be around for billions of years after we have gone. We are only here for a split second. But it is our second. Yours, mine and those we currently share the world with. It is the significance of insignificance. This is not a call to fill a dumb bucket list, this is a call to appreciate every moment. Drink in the air as though it were wine. Enjoy that grape as though it were an entire feast. When we wish for a different life, we are wishing for a false life.'

Dan searches the table again for another piece of paper. 'One of the words on that paper given to you was *Amor Fati*. I looked it up and it means 'a love of one's own fate'. The German philosopher, Nietzsche, once said, "My formula for greatness in a human being is *amor fati:* that one wants nothing to be different, not forward, not backward, not in all eternity. Not merely bear what is necessary, still less conceal it… but love it."'

She places the paper down in front of her and looks me dead in the eye, 'Fill your Cups, Frank. When you have full Cups, or know how to fill your

Cups, you will have joy, self-competence, autonomy, security, and self-worth – all of the outcomes of full Cups. Ensure your story is one of empowerment.'

Dan gives me another moment to ponder this.

'I think I need to clear my head,' I say. 'My mind's racing. Let me walk for a while.'

'Take your time, Frank,' she says. 'I'm not going anywhere.'

As I walk, I deliberate with myself, looking like a mad man talking to his wild hand gestures. At times, in my internal arguing, I am able to prove Dan's words to be wrong, but I quickly realise her arguments can stand up to what I am thinking. The most frightening part is how empowering this information feels. It's a scary moment when you realise just how much your decisions and way of thinking affect your world. What's more frightening is knowing that it's me that's maintained my suffering all these years. What's the saying? *Pain is inevitable, suffering is optional.* Taking that kind of ownership is heavy. It's like realising the shackles that bound you your whole life were never actually locked. That kind of freedom can be terrifying. Again, Jean Paul Sartre's *condemned to be free,* comes to mind. Free to think however I choose to. I am free to fill or empty my Cups by my own thoughts and actions. Nay, *I do* fill or empty my Cups by my thoughts and actions regardless.

I want to stop thinking for a while and contemplate stepping into a bar. Again, that would've been my choice. Instead, I order a takeaway cappuccino and sit down by the river. An hour passes, maybe more.

After staring off in contemplation for so long, my mind eventually works its way back to my wife's affair. I acknowledge now that I couldn't control what she did. All I can control is myself in this moment right now, and I've decided I'll no longer make that event part of my story. The funny thing is, I truly hope she's found peace. I don't wish her any malice. I truly hope she's been able to silence those inner demons of hers. However, I will not be punished for her crime any longer. I refuse to make it a Cup-emptying story.

These thoughts instantly release me from the agony I've been carrying around in my chest for the last twenty-odd years. And as the sun kisses my cheek, I feel peace.

I decide to make my way back to Dan's store. She greets me just as warmly as she had earlier that morning.

FRANK

18. ACCEPTANCE, MEANING AND GRATITUDE

'So, what else did you discover in your research?' I ask, sitting down at the table.

'Are you sure you want to go further today, Frank? We can pick it up tomorrow if you like?'

'No, I think I would like to continue if that's okay?'

Dan turns the kettle on and then reaches for her mug. With her back to me she slightly turns her head and pauses.

'Is everything okay?' I ask

Dan remains unmoved.

'Dan, is everything…'

'How would you feel,' she asks, turning to face me, 'about continuing this at the café?'

Though her voice sounds confident, lines form across her forehead.

'Ahh, yeah. I mean, yeah. Yeah sure, that would be perfect.'

With slow and deliberate movements, she walks towards the front of the shop, and I stand close by her side. We stop when we get to the front door. Dan takes a deep breath and unlocks it. I step out into the street first, and then Dan pokes her head out, looks back and forth, and then steps out. After locking the door, I offer her my arm, like a beau might at a dance, and slowly we walk towards the café. When we arrive, we make our way to the very back and sit at the table next to the one we sat at last time. Sitting down, with her back to the wall, Dan places two hands on the table and takes a deep breath.

'Okay… I'm good,' she says.

I don't want to leave Dan alone, so I wave at the young girl behind the counter, over-emphasising my own frailty to get her attention.

'How are you both today? Would you like a drink to start?' she asks as she slides some menus on the table.

We order our drinks and muffins, and dive back into our exploration of the Cups.

Dan closes her eyes and takes a few composing breaths. 'Okay,' she says. 'Where were we?'

'I was asking what else you found with your research.'

'Oh yes. Well, I found that unrealistic expectations are the enemy of acceptance and can also empty our Cups. Sometimes we forget that we all experience pain, heartache and loss. Every single one of us. I'm not saying we're not special, I am saying that we all experience painful setbacks. Sometimes we feel like we've been treated unfairly by things that could've occurred to anyone. What I think is we need to have more realistic expectations of the world we live in. This doesn't mean whatever happened to us doesn't matter, it just means our pain is universal. We don't get upset when it rains, because we expect rain, yet we get upset when we experience a late train. Trains are late every day, yet we are still surprised when it happens. Rather than spending our time expecting everything to always be fine, and things to always go our way, it's about accepting the world as it really is. Knowing that trains will be late, and painful events will occur…'

Those last words seem to touch a nerve with her as she looks around at her surroundings.

'The book you first held when you came into the store,' she says, 'in it there's a passage that reads: "Is a life without pain possible? Then don't ask the impossible." Asking the impossible leads to more unrealistic expectations and more suffering. That is why Bruce Lee said that we shouldn't pray for an easy life, that's unrealistic, we should pray to endure the world as it actually is. But remember, just as pain exists in the world, so does love and joy. In fact, you can't know one without the experience of the other.'

'This all sounds a tad pessimistic,' I say. 'Even Cup emptying, dare I say.'

A faint smile filters across Dan's face and she nods slightly. 'Well, I don't mean it in the sense that we should all go around with our heads drooped like Eeyore, waiting for Winnie and Piglet. I don't even mean it as in we should expect the worst to always happen. We just need to be mindful that it *can* occur. More in the sense that being forewarned is forearmed. Often, we get more upset about things when they take us by surprise. We're often more surprised than hurt, we just confuse the two and empty our Cups. Things that shouldn't surprise us do so because we have unrealistic expectations.

'Okay, what's an example?... Alright, imagine two people are at the airport and are waiting to catch a flight home to see their families. Now imagine the flight is suddenly cancelled last minute. The person who was certain they would be seeing their family that night would have their Cups emptied more than the person who anticipated this *could* happen. Planes get delayed every day. The person who knows it's a possibility is not taken by surprise, and therefore is not disarmed by it. It doesn't mean they were being pessimistic. They were just aware that it was a possibility. They held onto that bit of information so that when the event occurred it didn't disarm them. Therefore, the event will not be as Cup emptying for that person... Dare I take this one step further. If we understand that each day could be the last day we ever see a loved one again, which unfortunately will be true one day, we will appreciate that person more. If someone, however, always expects to see their loved one forever, they may take them for granted as always being around. It was Schopenhauer who said, "Mostly it is loss which teaches us about the worth of things." Again, this doesn't have to be gloomy. It's about understanding. It's about holding that information. It's about having realistic expectations.'

I think about this for a moment and, as usual, Dan gives me the space to do so. I guess having realistic expectations is neither negative nor positive if we don't make it emotive. Having realistic expectations, I suppose, is about seeing the world as it actually is and accepting the things outside of your control.

As though Dan is reading my mind, she says, 'Epictetus once said "Don't demand or expect that events happen as you would wish them to. Accept events as they actually happen. That way peace is possible." I also heard a quote somewhere that said the key to happiness is letting each situation be what it is, instead of what you think it should be.'

'So, what's the point of all this?'

'I think the point is the Will to Fill,' Dan says, as our drinks are placed on the table in front of us. 'Remember when we discussed *meaning* a little while back when we looked at Jean Paul Sartre, when researching the Freedom Cup? Like Sartre, the existentialist, Camus, also speaks of creating our own meanings. In one example he uses the myth of Sisyphus as a vehicle. Sisyphus was a Greek king, who, after cheating the persona Death, was condemned to spend eternity pushing a large boulder up a hill, only to have it roll back down to the bottom once he reached the summit. The king then returned to the bottom to perform the same task until the end of time. Camus is famous for comparing the plight of Sisyphus to our own sense of meaninglessness we experience from time to time. That day after day we roll our own boulders uphill. What Camus does do, however, is offer us some reprieve. He believes all we need to do is imagine Sisyphus is happy. If we imagine that he is happy, then he would have found meaning in his suffering. Sound familiar?

'Viktor Frankl also talked about finding meaning in suffering. When he found meaning in his suffering, he didn't bother to alleviate that suffering. We could also acknowledge that imagining Sisyphus happy is also acknowledging that it was up to him all along how he decided to *feel* about the situation. He couldn't control the situation, but he could control how he responded to that situation. Most importantly, I want to add this to the famous analogy by saying that not only should we imagine Sisyphus as happy, but he is also therefore creating his own meaning. What we can also acknowledge is that every time he reaches the summit, although it is only brief, he would enjoy that moment more than any other being who ever stood at that summit ever could. It might only be a moment, but all we ever have is this moment we are in right now. And in that moment, we know Sisyphus' Cups are full. As brief as it may be, he's found fulfilment.'

'So, in a sense,' I say, trying to work it out, 'rolling the boulder up the hill is equated to Cup filling.'

'Yes, and Cup filling gives us meaning if we are filling it authentically by living by our values and not affecting the rights and needs of others. Cup *filling* gives us fulfilment, even if it is only momentary. At the summit, we will experience joy, self-competence, autonomy, security, and self-worth. But most importantly, we will find a lack of want. No one else can give us this. It is only by rolling our own boulders – or filling our own Cups – that we can be fulfilled. Our Cups are our responsibility.'

I have a thought floating in my mind but, like an elusive dream, the more I struggle to recall it the further it slips away. I struggle with this for some moments, while Dan gives me space to do so, waiting quietly to answer any questions.

I am scared in a sense. She is saying things that almost detract from my own beliefs. 'Are you saying that we don't have any meaning outside of what we create for ourselves?' I ask.

'I'm saying I don't know if there's any grand meaning outside of what we make for ourselves. There might be, and I don't mean to offend you if you have spiritual beliefs. What I'm saying is those meanings are still, in a sense, beyond us. If you have faith, so be it, but create those self-affirming meanings for yourself as well. Basically Frank, the Will to Fill is filling whichever Cups require filling at that moment, filling Cups gives us meaning and fulfilment. We must always remember that our Cups are our own responsibility. Actually, I agree one-hundred percent with Schopenhauer, when he said, "It is difficult to find happiness within oneself, but it is impossible to find it anywhere else."'

'Part of me still doesn't quite comprehend exactly what the Will to Fill is. I mean, I get it in principle, but how does it relate to fulfilment?' I ask.

'The Will to Fill is only the unconscious internal driver, or *Will*, that motivates us to choose certain behaviours to fill our Cups. In short, it's the empty part of our Cups. Our dominant Cups require more to fill so that's where we usually see the Will to Fill. However, even our smallest Cups require filling, so if they are emptying, that is where the Will to Fill motivates us to fill those needs first. So, in terms of meaning and fulfilment, I think we need to consciously and skilfully fill our Cups.'

I scoop chocolate froth from my coffee and ponder what Dan said. A thought comes to me, 'Well, if we're naturally driven to fill our Cups anyway by the Will to Fill, why do we need to consciously fill them? Is it really that important if we are filling them consciously or unconsciously?'

'Good point,' she says. 'I'll have to think on that. Shall we take a break from all this theory, it's getting a little deep for one day.'

'How about once we finish these,' I say, pointing to our drinks, 'I take you back to your shop via the scenic route?'

Dan shakes her head, 'Not today, Frank. One day, perhaps.'

The next fifteen minutes remind me of the night Dan and I ordered in Malaysian food and spoke of everything and nothing. If my cappuccino was my Connection Cup, it would have spilt over into the saucer. Finally, we leave the café, and as we walk outside Dan pauses and looks around at her surroundings.

'You know what Frank? I don't think it could do too much harm just walking to the corner and back.'

It's the early hours of the morning when I hear my phone ringing. I look over at my bedside clock and, after my eyes adjust, I see that it's 3:20am. Who on earth would call at this time? Darlene? It must be an emergency. I get out of bed and walk into the kitchen where my phone is flashing, but as soon as I reach it the phone stops. Dammit. I scroll through to 'missed calls' as it starts ringing again. Dan's name flashes up on the screen.

'Hello?'

'Frank, I've got it. You know how today at the café you said if we are naturally driven to fill our Cups by the Will to Fill, why do we need to *consciously* fill them? I couldn't seem to let this go. I've been studying this since I left you today and I think I know why. Do you remember telling me how Sandi Phoenix said that Victor Frankl, the holocaust survivor, was self-actualising inside a concentration camp even though his other needs were not being met?'

'Yes,' I yawn, 'though I am also not one-hundred percent sure what self actualising even means.'

'Well, in a nutshell, it means reaching one's potential, or becoming your potentiality. Now listen to this…'

I can hear Dan rustling through her notes.

'… Okay, the psychologist, Carl Rogers, said that we have *actualising tendencies,* that *motivates* us towards *self-actualisation.* That is, actualising tendencies being an innate driver, or *Will,* even… So, we can see now that Viktor Frankl, showed *actualising tendencies* inside a concentration camp, even though his other needs were not being met. How is this possible, if his environment wasn't conducive to his development – as Carl Rogers believed it needed to be, to reach self-actualisation? I think Frankl, was using his *skills* in psychology as *behavioural choices* to fill his Cups. So, instead of Frankl being a slave to the Will to Fill, his *actualising tendency* combined with his skills purposefully filled his Cups. That is, he used his *skills* to *fill* his Cups... That's when the light bulb switched on for me Frank. Now listen carefully if that last part did not make sense. Self-actualisation is the *Skill to Fill.* The Skill to Fill is knowing the skills to develop a set of *behavioural choices* that will reliably ensure our needs are met. Self-actualisation therefore is the *process* of *active* Cup-filling, which requires skill. We could even assume that actualising tendencies therefore *arise* from the Will to Fill…'

Dan switches tone, knowing that I'm not completely grasping the philosophical and psychological jargon, nor making sense of it in context to our initial conundrum of why we need to consciously fill our Cups.

'So, going back, if we consider empty Cups as a kind of suffering that motivates us to fill our needs; Cups filled with ad-hoc behaviour, that is, without the Skill to Fill, is simply a momentary lack of suffering, as Schopenhauer would have put it. It might even cause us to choose thoughtless behaviours to fill one Cup that empties other Cups. The Skill to Fill, driven by the Will to Fill, however, is fulfilment. The Will to Fill drives us, but it's having the Skill to Fill that creates fulfilment.'

As always, as soon as I think I have grasped it, it seems to elude me. 'So self-actualisation is not actually about full Cups?'

'Correct. I see now that it's about Cup filling itself; the *process* of filling. The filling is the journey. Just as you don't read the ending of a book to feel fulfilled, you read the entire thing. It is the process that matters. Just as it was the process that allowed Sisyphus to enjoy the summit. The Will to Fill, is the internal driver. The Skill to Fill, is the method in which the Cups are being filled effectively… Let me give you an example, if your Safety Cup is empty, and on your way home you get junk food for dinner, you're not actually experiencing fulfilment, just a lack of suffering. Dare I say, even to the detriment of your other Cups as well. However, if you fill that need with a dinner that you prepared, or a carefully chosen meal to truly nourish you, then you're more likely to feel fulfilment, and for longer too. So, filling our Cups with thoughtless behaviour, is merely a momentary lack of suffering, but choosing to fill our Cups with our skills is a sense of fulfilment… I guess what I am saying is, to be self-actualising, we need to develop a set of skills to consciously and effectively fill each of our Cups. We need to determine our own unique Cups Profile and come up with our own individual Cup-filling plans.'

'Do you think there's a way we could always keep our Cups full?' I ask.

'I think gratitude can definitely help. On that topic, Marcus Aurelius mused to himself in his private journal, "Treat what you don't have as non-existent. Look at what you have, the things you value most, and think of how much you'd crave them if you didn't have them." What a great way of looking at things. He's showing us how to ignore the things we don't have by imagining they don't exist, and how to be grateful for the things we do have, by imaging how we'd feel if they were suddenly gone. I know sometimes I feel like my shop is a burden to upkeep, but I know if I were to lose it then I'd be devastated. It's by imagining it gone that reminds me to be grateful for what I have. Gratitude is the psychological adhesive that mends the holes in our Cups and helps keep them full for longer. So, I guess instead of always thinking about what we don't have, being grateful for what we do have and value in life helps keeps our Cups full… Frank, are you there?'

'Wait, I'm having a thought. To put it in Cups language, you could say gratitude is the ability to feel what is already in the Cup. In that case, fulfilment is the active acknowledgement and acceptance of the Will to Fill, while practicing the Skill to Fill, plus being grateful for what is already in your Cups.'

'I think you could be right.'

'What about death? Gratitude isn't immune to death. Surely that is the ultimate Cup-emptying experience?'

'Is it? Or perhaps after death there are no more Cups to fill? Either there is an afterlife, and you won't have to worry about your Cups anymore, or there is nothing. I didn't exist for billions of years before my birth and it didn't bother me one bit. Not existing for a billion years after I'm sure will be the same. I won't have any Cups to worry about… Look, Frank, all I know is that at this point in time the Phoenix Cups framework offers me the possibility of fulfilment. I say let's determine our Cups Profile. Let's find out which Cups are our dominant Cups, and which ones are smaller. Let's make a Cup-filling plan and choose to fill our individual Cups skilfully and authentically. Let's take control of this life of ours… Frank, it's by deciding to take back control of my life that I have decided I will be coming with you to the upcoming Cups presentation.'

'What did you say?'

'Once I knew I wanted to take ownership of my Cups and my life, I decided I had to go. I've even asked my nephew to join us. He makes me feel very safe… You see, Frank, I cannot control losing my husband, as much as I can't control what happened with my mugger. What happened has happened. It's done. I refuse to let it dictate my life and empty my Cups. My Cups are mine to fill.'

Although Dan spent the early part of the day basically saying the universe may be indifferent to our needs and desires, it suddenly feels as though the universe has shifted. My own personal universe, which takes place inside my mind – a place that is in everyone's minds.

'Dan, from the bottom of my heart I truly want to say thank you. Really, thank you. I've held onto the loss of my family for so long now that I've let it empty my Cups for long enough. I couldn't have come to this point of acceptance without your help. Your courage is giving me strength. I will always love my daughter, and I will do my best to connect with her and her son, but I know my Cups are mine to fill.'

'Getting a little sentimental there, Frank. Shouldn't you be sleeping?'

JACK

19. PAST AND PRESENT

The nurse enters the room. 'Frank, some of the patients are asking for you to keep it down. Do you mind lowering your voice a tad?'

Frank doesn't respond. Looking at my father's chest, I can see his breathing has shallowed.

'Young man,' I hear Frank say, ignoring the nurse. 'I won't begin to imagine I know the pain and disappointment that must've plagued your childhood. I won't begin to imagine that I know how that abandonment has later affected your life. Just know that what happened with your father was beyond your control. There's absolutely nothing you could have done to change anything. You can't go back and change your childhood, no more than you can change the movements of the stars. You can let go of any guilt you might have right now about not being close with this man, because that wasn't up to you. The thing is, son, you can't change your past but, also, you don't need to. Believe it or not, your past does not have to equate to your present. The consequences of holding onto that pain can be more grievous to you than the man who caused it. Hating this man who lay dying before you will not change a thing. All it does is empty your Cups.'

Beep.

My breath falls into my stomach. Do I really hate him? Maybe it isn't hate, maybe it's sadness. Maybe it's because it hurt too much to miss him, that I found it easier to hate him. My brother was right, my father did show me he loved me numerous times, it was just in ways I couldn't recognise.

'You know Frank, even though my only contact with my father was a birthday card and a one-week-a-year holiday, you want to know what the hardest part was? It was when he was driving me back to the airport. When you're a child, a year is an awfully long time between visits, and I always knew these were our final moments together. On our drive he'd try to cram a year's worth of advice into one car ride. The whole ride I would fight hard against the tears. I could always feel them building up behind weak walls, cracking now and then, letting little ones through. "Do well in school," he'd say. "Don't smoke. Never lie. Be humble..." By the time we'd park the car, it didn't seem to matter how hard I tried, the tears would stream. By the time we reached my gate, I'd be heaving and embarrassed. Not once, though, did my father shed a tear. Not once did I see any emotion ever filter across his face. I used to think he didn't care. Listening to you tonight Frank, and everything you've told me, even about how you held your tongue so your daughter wouldn't hurt despite how much it hurt you, I'm wondering if he too was holding some of my pain for me?... I guess I'll never know.'

Frank is quiet. Have I overstepped the mark? I notice that the rain has stopped, and all the lights in the hall are dimmed.

'You know,' Frank announces, 'one of the very last things your father said to me, I found very insightful. He said that he regrets everything. He regrets marriage, but more so he regrets divorce. He regrets spending so much time alone, but more so he regrets wasting so much time on others. He even said he regrets being born, but more so regrets dying. He did say, however, that his biggest regret of all was not spending enough time with his boys. Not showing you both how much he loved you. He had no counter regret for that one. I have no doubt that he held some of your pain at the airport when he dropped you off, but also that he regrets not shedding a tear'.

FRANK

20. THE PRESENTATION

The sheer size of the International Convention Centre dwarfs the entire city block, and the hallways bustle with people dressed in evening wear. Different lives, different Cups Profiles. In the hall outside the auditorium, I see the Phoenix Support stand. The man and the two women from last time are there again. I point them out to Dan, who's dressed in an elegant black gown, and Jackson who stands by her side as she grips his arm.

'Do you think we should go over?' I ask.

'Do you think it's necessary?' Dan replies.

'No. I suppose not. Let's find our seats.'

We find our places in the great auditorium, and my heart flutters in excitement that I get to share this moment with Dan. The lights go down. The rumble of conversation turns into a murmur. Every so often a Fun Cup could be heard giggling. Sandi Phoenix appears on the stage the way you might expect a rock star. I look at Dan and she smiles back.

'Hello everyone,' Sandi says into her microphone, and then proceeds to give a brief rundown of the Phoenix Cups for those who didn't yet know the framework. Behind her as she speaks is a diagram of the Phoenix Cup's model.

'You can't pour from an empty cup,' she says, changing the atmosphere in the room with her voice. 'As hard as I tried to, it's not possible. I could complain about all of the reasons why my Cups were empty. I could tell you how other people's alcoholism and drug abuse has affected my life. I could tell you how I am a statistic, one of the overwhelming number of women who were sexually abused before they reached adulthood. I could tell you how I became a Mum before I'd finished being a teenager. I could tell you how I chose partners who were more like DIY fix-it projects than relationships. I could also tell you how, like many women, I learnt to live with domestic violence, how to hide it, how to forgive it, and how to make excuses to stay, because leaving seemed just as hard. That "rock bottom" people talk about, that's what I found at the bottom of my empty Cups.

'One of my oldest friends once said to me that I could write a book about the madness that happens in my life. Ever since she said that, almost twenty years ago, whenever I'd find myself in an unreal situation that went from bad to worse, she'd just shake her head and say "Only you, Sandi. This could only happen to you."

'The truth is, though, we've all got our stories. Every one of us. We have words to describe them precisely because they're shared stories. We all live through a great deal of bullshit. To be honest, I am extremely grateful for my life. I was fortunate to be born with an able body, in a country abundant with all things Cup filling. I am fortunate that where I live there is no war, no famine, no madman for a president; nothing but my choices, and the awareness that I can choose how to view my story. So, my stories of the *tough times* don't define me. It's how we choose to live each day – regardless of those events – that has the most power over our lives.

However, there's one particular story that I want to share. I want to tell you about it because I know for certain it was a life-changing moment. Even more so than the events I mentioned before. Not because they were any less significant, but because this specific event put an end to a lifetime of living in directionless chaos. Like a compass that had been spinning in circles, this incident allowed me to find my northing arrow and start to move in a straight line.

'The tiny cottage we'd just moved into was bursting at the seams with stuff. Lots of stuff. So much stuff that packing boxes were stacked to the ceiling. My partner at the time, his two children and my two children had all just moved onto this lush acreage that had a home a few sizes too small. It was fine though because there were cows mooing across the road and a babbling creek out the back. I was going to make this work for us, for the children, and the little bundle on its way.

'As I stuffed school uniforms into the dryer on the porch of this tired old house, I felt just as run down. I was as tired and stretched and strained as the floorboards that creaked underfoot. I came inside, shivering, locking the back door as though it would keep the cold out. I found my laptop in a box under more boxes, heaved a textbook out with it, and cleared a spot on the lounge. As I sat there with my hands hugging my hot mug of chai and staring at my statistics assignment, I thought, *It's going to be a long night*. At least all of the children, and fortunately my partner, had settled to sleep quickly.

'The dead of the night came and went but I wasn't alone. The in-utero bundle was busy. It had been more than seventeen weeks and I was getting used to his presence, unexpected as it was. After a couple of hours, I eventually finished the assignment I'd been working on and took my exhausted body to bed where sleep came quickly. Only a couple of short hours passed when I woke suddenly. *What was that sound?* All my senses suddenly became alive as adrenalin coursed through my body like a powerful wave. Another huge bang and my body launched forward, ready for action. Strength was given to every atom of my being as I slammed my fist down on the baby's father's chest to wake him. My thoughts were racing, trying to move from dreamy confusion to reality. *Wake him up. He's strong. He can stop them. Can't he? Who are they? Oh my god, the children!*

"Get up!" I screamed.

'We were both at the bedroom door in a microsecond, and as he opened it a new wave of adrenalin hit me as we felt the hot force of an inferno slam us in the face. The fire was wild, noisy, hungry, uncaring.

"You deal with the fire. I'll get the kids," I heard myself say.

'I ran into the youngest's bedroom across the hall. His tiny three-year old body lay lifeless in his little car bed, just below a thick layer of glowing air. It wasn't until I picked him up that I realised he was sleeping soundly as the house burned around him. When he came to, I told him it would be okay as we ran down the hall for his siblings. I could hear them already screaming for me, and I for them. The fire was moving rapidly, finding its way into every room by breaking windows. A smoke alarm finally sounded. The smoke in the children's bedrooms was intensely dark, forcing me to rely on my other senses. I reached and felt all their arms in the darkness and pleaded with them to hold tight, telling them we needed to run for the front door if it was still there. The flames seemed to lick at us without touching. A scared little girl's voice screamed desperately as we ran past the kitchen, "It's already on fire!"

'My heart sank as I realised that's where I kept the key to the front deadbolt. *Had I locked the front door? Will it open?* It seemed hopeless to try, but we ran for the front door anyway. Nothing can describe my relief as the door – I'd carelessly forgotten to bolt it – swung open and fresh cold air washed over our faces. Outside, I pushed my stepdaughter down the three stairs and bundled her little stepbrother in her arms. It was then that I realised that somewhere along the way the other set of small arms must have lost their grip. Without thinking, I dived back inside the house and quickly found a head of scruffy hair attached to a little boy whose body was coughing and heaving. I took him to his siblings and told them to run to the tree and stay there. I counted them as they ran, just as I had counted them last weekend over and over again at the local pool while they played joyously, without a care in the world.

"One, two, three, four… wait. One, two, three… One, two, three… Where IS she? Dionne!" I screamed. My oldest. She's always late. Always taking her time. *Oh no, not this time. PLEASE not this time.* More waves of adrenalin, but it wasn't enough to get me back down that hallway. The smoke hit the back of my throat like a solid wall. I couldn't breathe. I needed a breath, just one. I turned back for the front door that was letting in cool clean oxygen. It was like putting my head above water and taking another dive. Then strong hands caught me at full sprint and hauled me out again. I fought him, he didn't know we were missing one.

"I can't find Dee! I think she's on the top bunk," I cried.

'He pushed me further away from the flames as he ran back into the unforgiving smoke. My body was in no state to wait. I sprinted to the back of the house, the part that was still standing. Somehow, my pregnant body climbed a metre off the ground to reach the window. My right fist loaded behind my head and came crashing down onto the window that wouldn't open. It cracked. My fist hit it again, and again, until it smashed. I then ripped glass out of the pane with my bare hands to make a hole in which I felt around on the top bunk. My hands searching for her body, my heart pleading to find her, I could hear her newly appointed stepfather inside searching for her.

"She's not here," he called to me. The desperation was tearing through me. I'd lost her. I kept fighting to get in through the window.

"She's not here," I could hear his voice again, this time getting further away as he knew it was now or never to leave the house. I pulled more glass out of the window trying desperately to get my body into that room. I was going to find her. I was not going to let this happen. This *cannot* happen to us. Then I felt hands from behind me dragging me down, and back to the earth as he repeated, "She's not here."

'His face was now in front of mine, and he was smiling. Why is he smiling? "She's not here. She's at her dad's house," he said.

'The world stood still as we looked to where all three children huddled together, under the tree. They were holding each other with wide fear-stricken eyes, waiting, crying... safe. Time froze for a moment as we realised we'd all made it out alive. Then a strange, bizarre, confused laugh erupted.

"Are we all really okay?" I asked.

"Yeah. I don't know how but we all made it out," he replied in as much disbelief.

Reality snapped back as our neighbours came running, shouting, "That's a gas bottle!" We hadn't even heard the hissing sound until now. One last wave of adrenalin coursed through me as I ran with the children further away to safety.

"I'm bleeding," squealed one of the children. I dropped to the ground to look her over, but another stroke of luck, the blood was not hers. "Eeeeew, your hand is all open," she said.

"It's fine, I can't feel it... I think we're all ok."

'The children shared my relief, looking intently at me so they knew how to react. I smiled. They smiled.

'When a paramedic arrived, he had a comforting face which deliberately ignored the biggest bonfire he'd ever seen so he could focus on the hand. That hand I recognised as my own but felt strangely dissociated from. He asked if I had any medical conditions.

"No. I'm good. I .... Wait," I ripped open the heavy blanket that was hugging me to reveal an obvious, neat little baby bump. We raced to the hospital in the ambulance as the sirens blared. There was no need for alarm though. The doctor was very pleased with the tiny human doing somersaults in my belly, who seemed to be behaving as though it was any ordinary sunrise. The nursing staff said we were all over the news and the radio. They gave their condolences, however, we smiled and told them there's no need. We're all okay. Everything else is just stuff.

'I'd love to tell you that we all lived happily ever after, but I'd be lying. Only three days later, I was hugging my brother-in-law, thanking him for letting us borrow his car. Before we even reached the emergency accommodation, however, we got a call from my partner's sister. She was screaming from the depths of her soul, telling us to come back to my brother-in-law's house. We got back in time to see the paramedics working on his lifeless body. They recreated a heartbeat, but he never came back. The coroner found a previously undiscovered enlarged heart, a congenital cardiomyopathy that meant this strong young father had been a ticking time bomb for the twenty-eight-years he'd been living.

'We'd been at the site of the fire for days, pulling out whatever charred memories we could find. But now this. I remember sitting in that worn hospital chair, looking at my sooty feet in borrowed thongs. We were waiting for the moment we would see the machines turn off and we would say our final goodbye to a sweet, kind, and loving man. Sitting there, I cried and cried and cried. Our support network that had been holding us up for the last few days now crumbled around us with the death of my unborn baby's uncle.

'By now we'd been on the evening news on all the commercial television stations, and the front page of several newspapers. I'd even been quoted in the local newspaper as saying, "It's only stuff. We're just so grateful we're not planning a funeral." And now we'd be planning a funeral.

'The evenings were the hardest, when my wonderful friends weren't around to wipe my tears and tell me, "You've got this". It was usually in these times I'd call the only other night owl I knew. Rexy, my partner's father, and the soon-to-be Grandfather of my youngest child. He and I would talk for hours as I sorted through bags of donations, making piles of clothes for the children, cleaning crockery, and generally keeping myself busy. An eccentric and grumpy old man, he had somehow become one of my closest friends. We'd talk politics, argue about philosophy, and we'd teach each other new words. I'd call him a hermit, while he would say my extroversion was exhausting.

'I can recall one particular evening with perfect clarity. I was sitting cross-legged in our temporary accommodation, and sifting through bags of clothes, when the phone rang. His voice immediately comforted the tears I'd been ignoring all evening, and he spoke these exact words:

"Sandi, sometimes I doubt my genius, but tonight I am absolutely certain of it."

'I laughed, as I wiped my wet cheeks and felt the relief of a smile. "Okay old man, tell me more," I said.

"I know what you need to name the baby. He has to be Phoenix. It's a mythical bird that rises from the ashes and…"

"I know what a Phoenix is, old man," I interrupted. I knew he would be able to hear my smile over the phone. "Far out, Rexy, you've nailed it."

'If we had it our way, it would've been the baby's first name, but his father insisted it be his middle name. And so it is. My little Phoenix had only been on the planet for a week when I completed my final three-hour exam for my degree in psychology. My massive Mastery Cup refused to take the leave the university offered me, despite my relatively empty Cups. My little Phoenix also came to my graduation months later.

'Since the fire, Rexy and I would often reflect on how that fateful night changed me. One of the biggest changes was where my bar was set for a so-called "bad day". Apart from the bad days I was experiencing living with an aggressively volatile partner, I've had very few bad days since. My perspective took a monumental shift. Also, my connection to "stuff" – like sentimental mementos, the newest TV, or lavish furniture changed. Essentially, "stuff" no longer filled my Cups. This was useful when a couple of years after the fire, I'd leave my partner with only the stuff I could fit in my supportive friend's car boot. When she'd found out what went on when he chose to get drunk, she insisted I live in her spare room until I could get back on my feet. Rexy was relieved – for many years he was the only person who knew.

'During this same year, I desperately needed Fun and Freedom Cup filling. One thing I knew was that the business I'd always dreamt of starting was no longer going to be a distant dream. I'd survived the impossible to live another day, and my brother-in-law's mortality had been the nail in the coffin; pardon the pun. I knew, though, that just existing day-to-day and planning for a future that might never come seemed a gross waste of time. Life is so startlingly short and can be taken away, or changed, gut-wrenchingly fast at any moment.

'The day eventually came when my compass stopped spinning and pointed north. So, after registering my baby's middle name as Phoenix, I started my business *Phoenix Support for Educators*, with a close friend and exceptional teacher. I now knew where I was going. I was a single woman, co-parenting children, growing a business, and living my dream. I finally dropped my married name and adopted my baby's middle name. I was as much a Phoenix as he was.

Looking back now on all those challenges, it all felt so unbearable while it was happening. Now I look back on that moment in time and realise that there really was no other way to become who I am today. Nietzsche once said, "How could you rise anew if you have not first become ashes?" I find it fascinating that it took losing everything to realise the value of anything.

'Posttraumatic growth is not an outcome, it is a process, and it takes time. Since meeting my husband and soul mate, Chris, five years ago, I am nothing short of a different person. I'm not saying I needed a husband to do that, but I can't deny his monumental part in getting me where I am today.

We share a purpose and keep each other on track. He reminds me that I have Cups other than just my dominant Mastery Cup, and he ensures I make plans to fill them too. The Phoenix Cups is a model that we've created together through living and breathing it. The shared language that it provides is imperative in exploring it further and gaining the many and varied perspectives of others. Since creating the Phoenix Cups, it has helped me understand my needs and the needs of others better, and life makes a great deal more sense now. I hope it does the same for you. I am also learning to be thankful for the privilege of growing older. My favourite old man left this earth just a few months ago. In his last days in hospital, nurses would ask my relation to him, I would proudly say "I'm his daughter-in-law."

"No, she's not, she's my best friend," Rexy would say.

'This is the first time I've told my story to an audience, and I'd always imagined he'd be here for that. It's difficult doing this without his uninvited, albeit excellent, advice. Before he passed, Rexy stopped saying "You look tired", or "Are you looking after yourself?" and replaced his fatherly concern with a joyous, "You look happy."

'I'm not just happy, I'm fulfilled. After all, you can't pour from an empty cup.'

FRANK

21. BLINDED BY THE LIGHT

I turn to Dan and see that her eyes glisten. Even her nephew is captivated by Sandi's story. The house lights brighten slightly.

'Let's think about your own Cups Profile now,' Sandi says.
'What do you think your dominant Cup or Cups might be? That is, which Cups are the biggest, so take the most to fill? It's important that your dominant Cups are filled frequently. But how do you identify which are your dominant Cups? You'll be able to determine this by the behaviours you choose. For instance, if your dominant Cup is Mastery, you're likely to be quite aware of your need to Master things or be in control of your world. If your Connection Cup is your dominant Cup, then you probably know that you need a daily dose of connection, love, friendship, or belonging. Some people don't identify with any one Cup, but rather feel like their Cups are similarly sized. It's important that we take care of our smaller Cups too, because often we neglect those. For example, even those with a small Fun Cup need fun, however, it takes much less to fill it than someone who has a particularly large Fun Cup. We can usually even determine each other's Cups just by viewing their behaviour across various settings. More than likely we all have a friend

who has a dominant Connection Cup, who usually needs more love and acceptance from us, than another friend who might have a smaller Connection Cup. Therefore, we understand that their behavioural choices are going to be different. For example, we'd probably expect more affection from our dominant Connection Cup friend, than we would from our small Connection Cup friend.'

Dan looks at me and nods, with a smile across her face.

'If you're having trouble determining your unique Cups Profile,' Sandi continues, 'there's a free quiz on our website to help you work it out. The size of your different Cups is quite static. It is genetic, and it rarely changes throughout your life. However, whether those Cups are full or empty is dynamic and might change day-to-day, or even moment-to-moment. Throughout our life, our environment, our physiology, our behaviours and the behaviours of others, and also our own thinking, all impact us and can fill or empty our Cups. So, if all behaviour is chosen to fill a Cup, we need to be thoughtful and intentional about this. We always choose to fill our Cups in our own unique way. These behavioural choices depend on our experience, brain maturation, skills, personality, knowledge about social expectations, desire to be considerate or cooperative, and even success using that strategy before. It's important to note that our behaviour includes not only our actions but our thoughts. As my husband often speaks about in his presentation for Workplace Wellbeing, you can choose Cup-filling or Cup-emptying thoughts.'

Sandi puts a link to the Phoenix Cups website on the screen behind her. Once Dan helps me navigate my phone, we all do the online quiz – including Jackson.

'What are your Cups, young man?' I ask him.

Jackson smiles into the luminous glow of his phone, 'Fun, then Freedom, then Connection, Mastery, and Safety comes last. What about you Aunty Dan?'

'Okay, I got Mastery, Freedom, Safety, and my Connection and Fun are equal last. How about you Frank?'

'I got Freedom, Connection, Safety, Fun, and finally Mastery.'

I left that Convention Centre transformed. It was as though someone had unchained me and led me out of the cave of darkness in which the world I thought I knew had only ever been dancing shadows. I was still adjusting to the new-found brightness as I could now see my own behavioural choices and the choices of others more clearly. From the Sandi Phoenix presentations, and all the work I had done with Dan, I could see why I had been so driven towards certain needs. I could also see how my drinking must have been affecting my daughter's Connection Cup. She chose the behaviour to stay away and fill it by connecting with others. People are simply trying to meet their own individual basic human life needs, which differ from one another. Instead of being in general disharmony, I'd now be able to pinpoint whatever it was I was lacking; which Cup I needed to fill.

FRANK

22. CHILDREN OF THE REVOLUTION

That evening, I find it hard to sleep. The moment I slip into that land between consciousness and sleep, Sandi's presentation starts to play over in my mind. I feel like a historian, piecing together the wisdom I gathered from Dan about not making life events my story, and how Sandi herself was able to transcend her past to create a future more fitting for her. One thing keeps jumping out, and that's this idea of moving forward. I guess one of the ways to move forward is making sure your anchor is up. *What's my biggest anchor?* I knew what I had to do.

I get out of bed and go into the kitchen and pour myself a whiskey. After a moment of staring at the glass, I pour it back into the bottle and grab a beer from the fridge instead. I open it, take a mouthful, and then sit on the couch. I get out my phone and dial a number. It rings four times before Jane answers.

'Frank. It's 11:30pm. What are you doing calling this late?'

'Sorry Jane. I just really needed to talk, to say a few things. Don't worry, it's not like the old days… First thing I want to say is, well, I am sorry.'

'That's great Frank. Can I go back to bed now?'

'Please Jane, just five minutes?'

I hear a sigh, 'Five minutes.'

'Do you remember when we first got together, and we would spend nearly the entire day just laying in bed, holding each other?'

'Frank...'

'No, Jane, it's not how it sounds. I'm not reminiscing trying to make you have those feelings again. I am making a point.'

Jane lets out another sigh, a universal sigh that says, *Continue, I guess.*

'What I remember the most from those days was your spontaneity. You were this spontaneous, unconventional free spirit. After laying in bed all day, how often did you wake me at two-in-the-morning with pancake cravings that sent us into the city? What I am saying is, you have always been a great big Fun and Freedom Cup.'

'Well, I guess I've been called worse names than a Cup before.'

'What I mean is you have a big need for Fun and Freedom in your life. More than I do. I just didn't understand your needs, and you didn't understand mine. When I thought that surely one of your Cups was full, because by that time mine would have been overflowing, that same amount in yours would've only half filled it. So, after the honeymoon period, those behaviours we initially were attracted to in one another, well, they started to bother us. Instead of understanding each other's needs, we annoyed each other. We neglected each other's needs. Or more importantly, we neglected our own needs which were up to us to fill.'

'Why are you saying all this?'

'I just want to acknowledge that I didn't always respect your needs, nor did you understand mine. No one's fault really, we just didn't know any better... But what I really want to tell you is, well, what happened that night – you know the night I mean – although that hurt more than I've ever been hurt, although I've carried this tender scar into every moment since that night, there's something I need to acknowledge, something I need to take ownership of… I have to admit that I no longer wanted to be in that relationship either. I don't condone what was done, but I have to admit that I wasn't the most attentive husband, and the end of that relationship really was the best thing for both of us.'

'So, what's this supposed to be, one of those moments where you call saying you forgive me, and expect me to thank you?'

'No, not at all. All I'm saying is that when we were young and in love, I loved you with every fibre of my being. And when our marriage ended, it did so because it was already over.'

'Why are you calling then Frank? Why are you telling me all this?'

'I'm calling you because although we have not loved each other for a long, long time, despite how it ended, and even with all the ups and downs, I am also really happy that we were happy once, which made it all worthwhile. I also just wanted to let you know that it makes me happy that you're happy now; that you have finally found the peace you've been looking for, and you are exactly where you are supposed to be. I am now finally where I am supposed to be too. And of course, without that time, we wouldn't have had Darlene.'

Jane falls silent. 'You still there Jane?'

'Yes.'

'It went quiet, that's all.'

'Look, Frank, that's all very insightful, and I am really glad you're finding peace too, but it's getting late.'

'Yes, yes of course… Before you go, can you pass on a message to Darl…'

'Frank, we cannot keep going over this.'

'Going over what?'

'Darlene…'

'Oh, I know, I know. I'm not asking for her new number, I just need you to tell her…'

'Frank stop. Thank you for accepting what happened to us, but one day you'll have to accept that Darlene can no longer be a part of your life. Don't keep asking. For your own sake.'

Over the sound of sniffling, the phone hangs up.

'You know, when I was eighteen, I wanted to be a police officer,' Dan says, when we meet at the café the next day. 'Of course, in those days there weren't many women officers. But I wanted that power. I wanted that gun on my hip, and all the authority it carried with it.'

'That's really funny,' I laugh, 'because all my life I've seen the police as oppressors. I always saw them as bullies who were supposed to serve people not intimidate them. How funny that my viewpoint aligns with my dominant Freedom Cup, and yours with Mastery. I wonder how many other careers align with people's dominant Cups? I think helping young people determine their Cups could help with career choice.'

Dan lets out a giant, distracting yawn. After a moment she says, 'So, I didn't get to sleep until around 4am. I took a handful of David's final journals and spread them out on the floor in my shop. I sat in the psychology and philosophy corner – David's corner. I stayed up all night, Frank. My poor, poor husband. I didn't know that he was actually very ill by the end, and he was going to die. He just didn't want death to beat him. He wanted to decide when he would go. He didn't want to tell me because he knew I would try and stop him.' Dan lowers her head. 'I know I said I was worried I may have forgotten what his voice sounded like, well, when I was reading those words, I could hear his voice in every sentence. And as painful as every page was, with some making me laugh, some making me cry, so far all of it has been very cathartic... I can't begin to tell you how much I miss him, Frank.'

Dan lets me put my hand on her shoulder, and I tighten my grip reassuringly.

'I also want to tell you, Frank, how much I have enjoyed your company, and this little journey into self-discovery we have been undertaking. I know we haven't known each other long but I can tell you're a good man, and I am glad to have met you. Let's make sure this is not the end. I need a good friend like you in my life.'

FRANK

23. PARTING WAYS

Over fifteen months have passed since that presentation, and although Dan and I stopped meeting daily, we still catch up frequently. Sometimes at her shop. Sometimes at the café around the corner. Sometimes at the park by the river. By the end of last month, however, we began to meet at nearby restaurants in the evening. We still talk about Cups frequently, but we've also expanded our world. We're able to let each other into our little eccentricities you usually save for life-long friends and loved ones.

On the last Saturday in November, Dan asks me to meet her at a Contemporary Fusion restaurant in the city centre. I find her already seated when I arrive. I see that her skin is bronzed, her eyes are gleaming, and her hair's down from its bun and rests across her bare shoulders. She looks every bit like Botticelli's Venus – if she stepped off her shell and was waiting patiently with a clutched purse.

'What's the occasion?' I ask Dan, over the noise of the crowd.

The waiter interrupts us and hands us a parchment paper menu. 'Can I start you off with any drinks?' he asks.

I shake my head, 'Just water for me, thank you.'

Dan raises her eyebrows at me, and a faint smile passes her lips. 'I'll have a water as well then,' she says, not breaking eye contact.

'One day at a time,' I say. 'It's definitely easier on the days my Cups are full and my needs are being met… So, what are we doing here?' I ask.

'It's been a wild ride hasn't it, Frank? I cannot begin to tell you how different my world has become ever since you walked through my door. I still remember the way you came in. There was something in your demeanour. You were somewhat timid, yet there was a euphoria that seemed to emanate from you. As odd as I thought you were, I felt inclined to listen to you. When you came through my door, you brought something with you. Something you didn't even know you were carrying. You brought a key with you, Frank. A key that would unlock my imaginary chains. For that I will be forever thankful you came into my life.'

'Well,' I say, 'it was your knowledge that was able to unpack all this. All I had when I came to you was this theoretical framework and a list of words scribbled on a piece of paper. You were able to expand upon it and help me apply it to my life. With your help, Dan, I've been able to accept the harsh realities of this world and still find meaning and fulfilment. Things I would never have been able to achieve without you.'

The waiter returns with our water.

'So, you brought me here just to say thank you?' I ask.

Dan shakes her head, 'I wanted to bring you to this restaurant because this is where my husband and I used to go. Of course, it wasn't an active young people's place back then, it was a small Italian restaurant. You know, red and white checked tablecloths… But I brought you here to say goodbye, Frank. I've put my store on the market. I am going to fill my Freedom Cup and travel the world again. Travelling actually fills all my Cups, Frank. My Connection Cup might be filled watching small village children playing in a stream. My Fun and Freedom Cup might be filled eating from some street market vendor that I find. My Mastery Cup might be filled making my way through the world on my own, doing things my way. And my Safety Cup will be filled just knowing that back here, locked in my bookshop, I was never really alive.'

I reach forward and grasp her hand, giving it a firm squeeze, and then retract it again.

'How will you fill your Cups, Frank?'

'Well, I am already. For my Fun and Mastery Cup, I've taken up the harmonica. I'm not sure my neighbours care too much for it – particularly when I add my Bob Dylan vocals. For my Freedom Cup, I've made it a point to visit a new café every day that I've never been to, and then explore the area. For my Safety Cup, I am wrestling with giving up the drink. And my Connection Cup, I let go of any animosity towards my ex-wife. There's no point holding onto hot coals, when I am the one getting burnt. And as for Darlene, I still try to contact her whenever I can to tell her that I love her, and always will to the end of my time. That's enough to fill my Cups.'

'How about we play our Cups game one last time?' Dan suggests.

'Brilliant.'

'Okay, what about our waiter?' she asks.

'Tough one, because he's playing a part. That is, he wasn't born a waiter, he's playing a waiter. Still, he seems meticulous. A tad domineering and was no nonsense when he asked what drinks we wanted… I would say dominant Mastery Cup.'

Dan smiles and her eyes turn into crescent moons, 'What about the person who checks reservations at the front?'

'Oh, easy. Huge Fun Cup. I can still hear her laughing from here. C'mon Dan, give me a harder one. Okay, I'll give you one. See that couple over there, those two guys? What are their dominant Cups?'

Dan studies them, 'I'd say they both have dominant Connection Cups because look how in love they are, staring deeply into each other's eyes, even after being married. The one on the right, the one whose wedding ring we can see, I think has a bigger Fun Cup because his smile is so much wider. The other man has a big Safety Cup, because he can't stop studying the menu between gazes.'

We filled our Cups over dinner with more stories, laughter, and incredibly spicy food. We exist only in that moment, not giving thought to the fact that this night would one day bring about sweet nostalgia. Though I did not care too much for the restaurant, that dinner would have to have been the greatest of my life.

'I guess it's time to say goodbye,' Dan says, and embraces me in a tight one-armed hug outside, on the street. 'Never forget the Will to Fill and Skill to Fill, Frank. Make sure you make a conscious effort to fill your Cups every day. And keep sharing that great big heart of yours. I'll never forget you, Frank.'

'Where are you going to go first?' I ask.

'Italy, then France, then Spain. I don't really know where exactly after that. Though there is still so much more of Asia I need to see, and places I promised myself I'd return to one day… Did you know that on average we have just over twenty-seven thousand days upon this earth? We could spend our limited days living in the past or imagining some unrealistic future. Or, we could ground ourselves in the present, and be mindful of what we do have. Remember, there is no dress rehearsal. This is it. Right now. Each moment that passes is gone forever. Shakespeare so famously proclaimed through a despairing Macbeth, "Out, out brief candle." Worrying and complaining doesn't stop the undesirable, it just prevents us from enjoying the moments that do matter. We can either take control of ourselves and what we want, or we can be a victim of circumstance. No matter what we choose, that candle wick continues to burn. Indeed, one day that candle must go out, so until then I say, burn bright, and fill those Cups.'

JACK

24. THE END IS THE BEGINNING IS THE END

Beep.

Beep.

Beep.

'Last I heard she was in Sicily. I don't know if this was a year ago, or five years ago. Time confuses me a lot these days.'

Beep.

'You know, young man, I've shared a bed next to your father for weeks now. And I can tell you, when he was awake, it was always in the dead of night that I would hear him. He never said a word during the day, but late into the night he would weep for his boys. Now the story I told you tonight, one night while your father was at the depths of his despair, I told him that story. Like yourself, he didn't say much. I can tell you now though, son, that before he stopped speaking, he understood. He came to the same realisations that we all do who come to learn about the Phoenix Cups... He now faces what we all must face one day. Believe me, when I say to you that he is ready. Rest easy, young man. Although we don't always get to hear the words we need to hear, he never could have filled your Cups anyway. Only you can do that. You can even do that right now. You see, the scars might never go away, but you can learn how to walk with a limp. And no limp has ever stopped the sun from shining. Son, if you take only one thing away from our conversation tonight, know this: I can tell you without a doubt in the world that your father did indeed love you.'

At first my chin tightens. Then it quivers. Before I know it, tears stream down my face. My palms cover my eyes, and my body trembles. Frank is right. You can't control the situation, but you can control how you respond to the situation. You can control the levels of your Cups by the way you think about them, or by the choices you make. It's not up to life, or circumstance, it's up to you. Your Cups are your own, and only you can fill them. So, I accept now that I cannot control my past, and unfortunately, I can never fully repair my relationship with my father. But I can forgive him and fill my Cups.

The nurse appears on Frank's side, 'Okay Frank, my shift is nearly over. The morning staff will be here soon.'

'Goodbye, my dear,' I hear Frank say to her.

'Good lord, goodbye sounds so formal and final, Frank.'

The nurse comes over to my side, 'I'm about to finish my shift. Is there anything else you need before I go?'

'Yeah,' I say. 'Is Frank's daughter over there with him?'

The nurse smiles and shakes her head. 'He speaks to her often, but she's not there.'

'Has she come to see him at all?' I ask.

'No. It's not possible.'

'Why?' I ask.

Leaning in close, she says, 'She passed away some time back. Her child now lives with her grandmother.'

Oh, Frank!

After the nurse leaves the room, I notice the sun rising. Everything it touches seems to turn to gold. Even the wet car park is now black with gilt streaks. As the sun rises, the sky pales.

'I'm tired,' Frank says. 'I'm looking forward to closing my eyes. You know Mark Twain? Well, he once said, "Just as a happy day brings happy rest, so too does a happy life bring happy death." I'm not saying I've necessarily lived a happy life, or that "happy" is even the right word. Nowadays we look to be unnaturally happy, and become concerned if we're not. I've learnt that it doesn't matter. What is safe to say is in this moment, sharing my story with you, my Cups are full. I feel fulfilled, and I am ready to close my eyes.' With that Frank stops speaking.

My father's face suddenly looks more real to me than it has in years. Somewhere beneath the signs of aging, I can see the face of the man who used to drop me off at the airport. I see my hand reach out and push the hair off his forehead.

Beep.

Beep.

Beep.

> **BEHAVIOUR IS THE MIRROR IN WHICH EVERYONE SHOWS THEIR IMAGE.**
>
> JOHANN WOLFGANG VON GOETHE

BIBLIOGRAPHY

Aurelius, M. (2006). *Meditations.* London: Penguin Classics.

Boniwell, I. (2012). *Positive Psychology in a Nutshell: The Science of Happiness.* New York. McGraw-Hill

Brown, D. (2016). *Happy: Why more or less everything is absolutely fine.* Suffolk: Bantam Press

Camus, A. (2000). *The Myth of Sisyphus.* Great Britain. Penguin Books.

Chapman, G. (1992). *The 5 Love Languages.* Chicago: Northfield Publishing

Cox, G. (2011). *The Existentialists Guide to Death, the Universe and Nothingness.* Great Britain: Bloomsbury Publishing

Connell, M. (2016) *Stoic Comedy.* [Apple Music]. Available at: https://music.apple.com/gb/album/stoic-comedy/1115084804

Csikszentmihalyi, M. (2008). *Flow: The Psychology of Optimal Experience.* New York: HarperCollins.

de Botton, A. (2000). *The Consolations of Philosophy.* Italy: Penguin Books.

de Botton, A. (2016). *The Course of Love.* Australia: Penguin Books.

Foucault, M. (1977). *Discipline and Punish: The Birth of the Prison.* Great Britain: Penguin Books.

Frankl, V. (2004). *Man's Search for Meaning.* Great Britain: Ebury Publishing.

Glasser, W. (1998). *Choice Theory (1st ed.).* New York: Harper Perennial.

Harris, R. (2007). *The Happiness Trap: Stop Struggling, Start Living.* Wollombi: Exisle Publishing.

Irvine, W. (2009). *A Guide to the Good Life: The Ancient Art of Stoic Joy.*

New York: Oxford University Press

Jeffers, S. (2012). *Feel the Fear and do it Anyway.* London. Ebury Publishing.

Kaufman, W. (1976). *The Portable Nietzsche.* Unites States of America. Penguin Books.

Kierkegaard, S. (1992). *Either/Or: A Fragment of Life.* Unites States of America. Penguin Books.

Kierkegaard, S. (1985). *Fear and Trembling.* England. Penguin Books.

Klein, D. (2012). *Travels with Epicures.* Melbourne: Text Publishing.

Maslow, A. (n.d.). *A theory of Human Motivation.* Wilder Publications.

Maslow, A. (2011). *Toward a Psychology of Being.* United States of America: Wilder Publications

Nietzsche, F. (2003). *Beyond Good and Evil.* London: Penguin Books

Nietzsche, F. (2004). *Why I am So Wise.* London: Penguin Books

Nietzsche, F. (n.d.) *Thus Spoke Zarathustra.* London: Penguin Books

Paunch, R. (n.d). *The Last Lecture.* [online] You Tube. Available at: https://www.youtube.com/watch?v=ji5_MqicxSo

Pigliucci, M. (2017). *How to Be a Stoic: Ancient Wisdom for Modern Living.* Great Britain. Penguin Books.

Porter, L. (2014). *A Comprehensive Guide to Classroom Management: Facilitating engagement and learning in schools.* Australia. Allen & Unwin.

Porter, L. (2013). *Young Children's Behaviour: Practical approaches for caregivers and teachers.* Chatswood. Elsevier.

Phoenix, S. (2017). *The Phoenix Cups Framework: An Educators Toolkit for Behaviour.* Brisbane: Phoenix Support for Educators Pty Ltd

Phoenix, S. (2019). *The Phoenix Cups My Cup Filling Plan.* Brisbane: Phoenix Support for Educators Pty Ltd

Phoenix, S. and Phoenix, C. (2019). *Home.* [online] The Phoenix Cups. Available at: https://phoenixcups.com.au/

Plato and Waterfield, R. (n.d.). *Symposium.*

Psychology Tools. (2019). *Unhelpful Thinking Styles - Psychology Tools.* [online] Available at: https://www.psychologytools.com/resource/unhelpful-thinking-styles/

Sartre, JP (2003). *Being and Nothingness.* London: Routledge.

Sartre, JP (2007). *Existentialism Is a Humanism.* New Haven: Yale University Press.

Sartre, JP. (1965). *Nausea.* Great Britain. Penguin Books.

Schirmacher, W. (2010). *The Essential Schopenhauer: Key Selections from the World as Will and Representation and Other Writings.* United States of America. HarperPerennial.

Schopenhauer, A. (1970). *Essays and Aphorisms.* Great Britain. Penguin Classics

Schopenhauer, A., Carus, D. and Aquila, R. (2016). *The World as Will and Presentation.* London: Routledge.

Tedeschi, R. and Calhoun, L. (2004). *Posttraumatic Growth: Conceptual Foundations and Empirical Evidence.* Psychological Inquiry, 15(1), pp.1-18.

West, S. (2019). *Podcast. [online] Philosophize This!* Available at: http://philosophizethis.org/category/episode/

Wilde, O. (2003). *The Picture of Dorian Gray.* Great Britain: Penguin Classics.

Yates, R. (1989). *Eleven kinds of loneliness.* New York: Vintage Books.